T0198683

THE SOUL FOOD MUSEUM STORY

Volume I

Celebrating 400 Years of Culinary Arts Hospitality and Agriculture

CHEF KENNETH WILLHOITE

authorHOUSE®

AuthorHouse™
1663 Liberty Drive
Bloomington, IN 47403
www.authorhouse.com
Phone: 1 (800) 839-8640

Published by AuthorHouse 09/28/2018

ISBN: 978-1-5462-2515-7 (sc)
ISBN: 978-1-5462-2514-0 (e)

Print information available on the last page.

DEDICATIONS TO OUR ANCESTORS & GIFTS FOR GENERATIONS TO COME

"Nobody does it better" is a strong statement, but it may even be an understatement when it comes to the indelible impact and undeniable contributions that African Americans have made to the culinary arts in America. More specifically, the good things that our mouths are satisfied with daily would not be as special as they are, had it not been for the meticulous involvement of our ancestors.

Not only did our ancestors build this country where countless individuals come to discover and live out "the American Dream", but we have also tantalized the taste buds of the masses for over 400 years. In so doing, God has endowed us with a unique ability to make something out of nothing. Those things that "Massa" viewed as scraps from the dinner table were turned into delicacies that have been treasured and passed on from generation to generation.

Indeed, we've got much to be thankful for. However, it is not enough to leave our gratitude on the table. The colossal role that we contributed to society in culinary arts should never go unnoticed; it absolutely must be documented. In *400 Years of the History of Soul Food and Hospitality*, Chef Dr. Kenneth Willhoite has left no stone unturned as he takes us on a colorful journey from the coasts of West Africa to the hills and valleys of America.

The very essence of who we are as a people is finely and intimately woven into the tapestry of the details of this fine work of art. The 40+ years Chef Dr. Willhoite has spent collecting artifacts and chronicling every piece of history he could amass have produced the treasure which you now hold in your hands. What you are about to experience is nothing less than a masterpiece! By the time you complete this journalistic experience, be assured that you will be enlightened, elated, enthused, and empowered.

Therefore, prepare your hearts and minds to experience an adventure like no other. Without question, Chef Dr. Willhoite has raised the bar and laid a foundation that will allow our contributions to forever be inscribed in the pages of history...even if that means we must tell it ourselves. Chef Dr. Willhoite, thank you for telling the story. Thank you for a job far beyond well done!

King & Queen of Soul Food Chef Kenneth Willhoite & Queen Vida

FOREWORD

CHEF QUEEN VIDA AMUAH OF GHANA, AFRICA
After 400 years of captivity as Black people, we continue to thank the Omnipotent God of Creation for delivering us out of slavery as was prophesized in scripture – Deuteronomy 28:68 says

"And the Lord shall bring thee into Egypt again with ships, by the way whereof I spake unto thee, thou shalt see it no more again: and there ye shall be sold unto your enemies for bondmen and bondwomen, and no man shall buy you"
Kings James Bible Version – Public Domain

The mysteries of the Bible would be revealed in their set seasons and times.

African Americans have indeed fulfilled the prophecies as it is written in scripture. It is considering this, that Chef Dr. Kenneth Willhoite has worked night and day to celebrate this historic 400-year journey of an extraordinary group of people who, against all odds, fought to get their freedom. It took knowledge and vison – *without vision the people perish.* Chef Dr. Willhoite has diligently researched for over 40 years to tell the African American Soul Food Story, tracing our journey from Ghana, Senegal, Gambia, and many locations along coastal West Africa.

We must now use the knowledge passed on to us because this knowledge will give us the power to continue to be free. We must keep our destiny in our own hands. With love and gratitude, I am

Queen Vida Amuah, Queen of Soul Food
Ase - Oh, Ase
Peace and Blessings, Shalom

Contents

BOOK SUMMARY

THE SOUL FOOD MUSEUM STORY
AUTHOR – CHEF DR. KENNETH WILLHOITE

The Soul Food Museum Story is an historic journey of the African American culture through their passionate relationship with food. This book follows that special love of food and family from their roots in coastal West Africa to North and South America and the Caribbean. The Soul Food Museum Story paints a vivid picture of this horrific journey survived by extraordinary strong and resilient people, and their ability to recreate themselves and their culture despite all hardships and struggles.

This book will enlighten and educate on the complex history of soul food, an understanding of culinary arts (the art of preparation, cooking and presentation of food), hospitality (all forms of generous reception and entertainment of guests, visitors or strangers), and agriculture (the science of farming, including cultivation of soil for growing crops and other products).

Founder and Visionary for The Soul Food Museum – Chef Kenneth Willhoite

Organization founded in 2002 as way of documenting 400 years of African American History and presenting knowledge for the next generation.

"Losing My Goal Means Losing My Soul"

INTRODUCTION

This book is an act of love, dedicated to my African American ancestors. I will take the reader back through time, over the past 400 years, sharing the history of soul food via its historical journey from Africa to the Americas – North and South and the Caribbean. This will be an emotional and hopefully enlightening journey through time as we stroll together through my virtual historical museum.

Memories and the stories from the mouths of ancient elders was the only way that our African American culinary histories and contributions to mankind were passed from one continent and one generation on to the next. These stories still exist because of the power of our oral history. Not only were recipes passed from one relative to the next, but also their inventions, agricultural contributions, and folklore related to the many soul food dishes that we now know and love. They have almost become a part of our DNA. When many speak about their ancestor's favorite dishes, those memories are relayed with so much passion, honor and love.

This book is a mirror of our past – a past that has been overshadowed and ignored for too long. Many have taken up the mantle to tell their soul food stories in many different ways –all informative and interesting. The culinary contributions of African Americans have been chronicled in over 500 published cookbooks, in documentaries, in blogs, magazines and in encyclopedic reference books that help tell this unique African American story.

For more than thirty years, I have been searching every library accessible for pertinent information concerning and connected to African Americans in the culinary arts and hospitality industry past and present, hoping to add a view of the soul food journey that peaks the interest even further regarding our soul food story. I have included the voices of slaves who survived to share parts of their journeys that are so important to the transformation of food ways in America. My focus is directed toward unique and sometimes overlooked stories and information.

Beginning in 1619, almost 400 years ago, African families were forcibly removed from their homelands – never to return. Facts that I uncovered on my stroll through my ancestor's culinary history were sometimes painful, often extraordinary, and truly remarkable considering the hardships and struggles that African Americans suffered along this journey.

My hope is that this book will help change some negative images of soul food as an unhealthy threat to our culture because soul food encompasses more than what the eye can see and what the tongue can taste. As I share more knowledge and positive information to teachers, students, and people throughout the world with this publication, I trust that more people will then understand how African American culinary arts and hospitality contributions have positively changed the face of America.

It is my ultimate dream to use this book as a foundation for the creation of a permanent home for the Soul Food Museum, which would house other books, memorabilia, and examples of the history of soul food in America. Over the past years, I have devoted so much time and energy to building towards this dream. Every small step brings me a little closer. To some, my vision to build this museum may seem a little crazy and unreachable. But, how often has that been said about 'crazy' dreamers – from Orville Wright to Steve Jobs. Therefore, I will keep following this vision to its ultimate reality. My goal for such a long time has been to tell this story – the good, the bad and the ugly. I feel this is a divine assignment from God – it has become deeply embedded in my spirit – deep in my soul. *Therefore, losing my goal will mean losing my soul.*

The foundation for The Soul Food Museum began in the Annex of **Big Bethel AME Church** – the oldest African American Church in Atlanta. This foundation in the church seemed most appropriate to me because my initial vision came from God when, as a little boy, I heard the message that my connection with food – growing it, nurturing it, cooking it and just loving it – was what I was born to do. I knew then that it was my destiny, my purpose, and my mission to be a messenger for the soul food industry. So, despite life's challenges, I have stayed on my path with the wind of my ancestors continuously at my back.

From Big Bethel AME church, I moved my Soul Food Museum to a small building on historic Auburn Avenue in Atlanta where my collection of African American culinary artifacts began to grow with my continued research, collection and preservation of as many historical items related to the African American culinary experience that I could uncover. My dream is that The Soul Food Museum will become a support system for chefs, cooks, waiters, waitresses, bartenders, housekeepers, caterers, restaurateurs, hotel owners, food manufacturers, and more. Credit must be given where credit is due; we must take the responsibility for telling our own stories and I have taken on the task to tell our soul food story from my own perspective. The Soul Food Museum is now a mobile unit, awaiting its permanent home of brick and mortar.

In the beginning, God created the heavens and the earth. Now the earth was formless and empty, darkness was over the surface of the deep, and the Spirit of God was hovering over the waters.

And God said," Let there be light", and there was light. God saw that the light was good, and he separated the light from the darkness

Genesis 1: 1-4
King James Version – Public Domain

So, travel back with me, from the beginning in the very first garden - the Garden of Eden. This was a place of purity, filled with all good things from God's good earth – there to nourish the body and the soul. That was the germination of our true Soul Food. For African Americans, however, our journey has been historically marked just a short four hundred years ago, beginning with the horrific transport of unsuspecting human beings by Europeans across a giant ocean to North and South America and the Caribbean. With this transcontinental transport also came plants, seedlings, and other foodstuff that was indigenous to the African continent. These Africans also brought with them invaluable knowledge of how to grow and cultivate foods unique to their native homelands.

With bondage came a creative transformation of these slaves. Thrown into a hellish foreign environment, my slave ancestors managed to rebuild their lives based on that which they already knew and loved. This rebuild included their families – those that survived and those that became family because of circumstances. It also included their music – that served to help them maintain a unique method of communication and to help them to keep their sanity; and finally, this was the foundation for new and unique methods of cooking their food – which enriched this country as a whole. African Americans were creative and inventive problem-solvers in science, culinary arts, agriculture and hospitality. When Africans arrived in this new world, they used their indigenous knowledge to solve many of the problems facing a very young America, struggling to find its way and new independence. I find it so incredulous that a country built on "liberty and justice for all" would rob an entire culture of people of their own independence. But despite that oxymoron, Africans brought to this country managed to reinvent themselves into a new being – stronger, more resilient, and more determined to survive than ever before.

The story of soul food has been told and retold, many times over. And what will one more book about soul food offer? This book will be your journey through a colorful, historical museum filled with stories, images, and people who love what soul food has given them – an unspoken unity and ability to continue to exist, despite all odds. Those in this book, both the ordinary and the famous, have shared a common joy -- experiencing the ingenuity, creativity and culinary gifts given to them by God. I believe in all things that make us creatively unique. Those who have forged the way are such positive role models, and as an African American male, I know the importance of continuing to produce more positive leaders in our communities.

I pray that my message is heard, that lessons will be learned, and that the soul food story will continue to be shared with many. Since the 1860's, following the emancipation of slaves in America, African Americans have continued to reach higher and farther than ever, to achieve unending achievements in culinary arts and hospitality. In addition, people of color must continue to use every opportunity offered to them to create new pathways where none previously existed.

I feel that it is in divine order that on my birthday, January 8th of 2018, President Donald Trump signed into law **Bill # HR 1242 (congress.gov-HR1242) that celebrates the 400 years of African American history. With the creation of this bill, this history commission was established to develop and carry out activities throughout the United States to commemorate the 400th anniversary of the arrival of Africans in the English colonies at Point Comfort, Virginia in 1619.** The commission must do the following:

- Plan programs to acknowledge the impact that slavery and laws that forced racial discrimination in the United States.
- Encourage patriotic, historical, artistic, religious, economic and educational organizations to organize participate in the anniversary activities.
- To assist States locally to further commemorate this important history.
- To coordinate for the public, research relative to African American history.

It is no accident that the completion of my book coincides with the addition of this most significant law of our land.

"It cannot be said that we have not and do not contribute to society. Dreams do come true."

Chef Dr. Kenneth Willhoite

This is only the beginning of my journey – there are many volumes to come.

ORIGINS OF SOUL FOOD

In an article written by Creative Loafing Magazine writer Rodney Carmichael, I was referred to as "The Soul Food Missionary" because I have spent the last thirty years building a legacy of history, chronicling the stories of soul food in the Americas, beginning centuries ago with African Griots then, over generations, transitioning into modern day cuisine. Soul Food still embodies all the love that is found in preparing and enjoying the foods of extraordinarily determined, creative and resilient people.

The mere words "Soul Food" can, in some people, dredge up sights, feelings, smells and tastes of down home African American southern cooking, steeped in memories of festive family gatherings, with endless stories told by those we remember with love, around abundant tables of food. Every culture has its soul food, but they just call it by other names.

Initial references to Soul Food or "Food for the Soul" had a religious connotation, long before it became a term that stirred up thoughts of mouth-watering foods created by African Americans. One writer poetically referred to the Islamic prayer book as *"Food for the soul" … It is their hymn and their history"*[1] That describes, so beautifully, for me all that our Soul Food journey has become – ***our hymn and our history – our song and our story***, told generation after generation without ceasing.

My journey, and those of my ancestors who ended up in a very small town in Oklahoma, has often been a tough one. But my grandmother raised a dreamer, and she nurtured my dreams just like she taught me to nurture that which comes from the earth.

I have fond memories of watching my grandmother fix our favorite Soul Food dishes like collard greens, cornbread, ham hocks, yams, mac & cheese and more, that still warm my heart to this day. Just remembering the taste of her hot buttery cornbread, my absolute favorite mouthwatering treat, stirs up so many warm memories. I think back on all those smells and sounds coming from my grandmother's kitchen. It was like having Thanksgiving every day! Soul Food is certainly all about love for me, and my memories all relate to the creation, gathering, processing and cooking of so many wonderful things all from nature – from God, who has been providing for us since Adam and Eve.

---

[1] Humanism in Islam e-book by Marcel Boisard

GARDEN OF EDEN

Then into it, he blew the breath of life,
*And man became a **living soul.***
Amen. Amen.
From the Poem – **THE CREATION** by James Weldon Johnson

We were left with a **Garden of Eden** right here on earth, and it's still here for us if we choose to cultivate, maintain, and nurture it every day we live, with our own hands, and, of course, all of it done in love.

When I was just a little boy, I had a revelation from God. I so clearly heard a message from a source that I KNEW was God who told me that it was my destiny, my purpose, and my mission to promote the richness of my people through my love for the many culinary jewels from the earth. My mother planted in me the spirit of a fearless leader – to fear no one but God. That seed planted by my mother has helped me to stay the path and continue to live out my purpose and mission, letting nothing stop me from finishing this journey.

For me, there is nothing more spiritual than spreading seeds (literally and metaphorically), planting, then watching the fruits of that effort take form into wondrous gifts that can feed us for an eternity. We must, however, plant, nurture, grow, and harvest in unity as a people. But, unfortunately, we seem to be losing sight of that gift. So, following my instructions from God, I have, for the past forty years been working toward that goal – to tell everyone I can, in every way I can, that we still have fields to plow, seeds to sow, and harvests to gather.

The story of my people – African Americans – is one long and complex saga filled with twists and turns that have choked the life out of many, but has motivated so many more to far surpass the horrors of their painful past.

In my thinking, the meaning of "Soul Food" goes far deeper than just the cooking. As in references to African American music, particularly the music of the 1940's, 1950's and thru the 1960s, when jazz was King in the world of music and Black music was referred to as soulful, food prepared by African Americans evoked that same kind of soulful feeling. It was about this time that the words *"Soul Food"* took root.

What we have come to know as soul food, however, has its true roots specifically from the West coast of the African continent, then transitioned to North America, South America and the soulful magic of the Caribbean, all populated with those who came from the continent of Africa.

The 'soul' in the expression "Soul Food" implies a deep emotional response and feeling to the mere experience of cooking and in consuming foods that have a strong identity to whom we truly are – a blend of magical spices -- sugars, grains and starches that take the bland out of ordinary foods and ordinary ways of enjoying life. I believe that is what we, as a culture of people, have added to this country -- a special kind of spice that took the bland out of America. True "Soul Food" comes from the good earth and then is prepared by the hands of people who love so much those foods that come from nature, from creation, and from God. Soul Food takes the joy of gathering and preparing foods to a whole new level – a spiritual one that feeds the body and the soul.

Winding back the clock about 400 years to when we first set our shackled and bloody feet on these American shores – from North America to the Caribbean - the spirit of a stolen tribe of people was anything but soulful. But, my ancestors had bent, but not broken spirits. Their inner spirits were still full of strength, resistance, love of God, special knowledge and talents born into them from the time of their Egyptian ancestors, and creativity from their various homelands. Deliberate control of plant productivity dates back to 70,000 years ago in Southern Africa, and the world's earliest known, centrally organized food production system was established along the river Nile 15,000 years ago. The Nile River is the longest river in the world. This knowledge of agriculture would prove to be a great tool of strength for Africans brought to this land. Land is a universal concept because it is everywhere on this planet, and Africans easily transferred their knowledge and skills when transported to this country. And despite mistreatment, separation of their families, humiliation, and subjection to pure hatred from those who controlled them and treated them as less than full human beings, my ancestors overcame all that bound them. With song, with prayer, with ingenuity, my ancestors took what was meant to break them, and created a whole new culture of people, transforming from Africans to African Americans – filled with a new music, a new spirit, and a new food that for centuries has fed our souls.

BEGINNINGS OF THE SOUL FOOD CULINARY JOURNEY – FROM COASTAL WEST AFRICA TO AMERICA

Africa, said to be the cradle of all civilization, provided the seedlings for the culinary culture of a tribe of people who had to reinvent themselves when they were removed from their native land and then shipped like cattle to a foreign land filled with extreme mental, emotional, physical and culinary differences that would have broken many others. However, these Africans were made of strong stuff.

The **'Middle Passage'**[2] is a short term long associated with the transatlantic slave trade between Europeans in the East and Europeans who has settled in "The New World" across the Atlantic Ocean; but that has a very long and complex history. One colony at a time, Europeans settled in the Americas along the Atlantic Coast and claimed territories that reached down to the islands of the Caribbean.

During its three centuries of operation, the Atlantic Slave trade removed approximately 11.7 million people, mostly from West and Central Africa, with the intention of settling them as slaves in Europe, America and the Caribbean Islands. Only 9.8 to 10 million made it to their destination. The rest died in port, at sea or upon arrival in the new land.

---

[2] Middle Passage - The **Middle Passage** was the stage of the triangular trade in which millions of Africans were shipped to the New World as part of the Atlantic slave trade.

Africans began to arrive in the Americas more than a century before the landing of the Mayflower landed at Plymouth Rock or the Dutch settled in Jamestown, Virginia. But beginning in 1619, captured Africans, began the experience of a horrific and life changing passage across the Atlantic. On any given day in the early 1600s on the West African coast, any one of, or an entire family were being snatched from their villages, chained and dragged through dense woods to an unknown destination. Along the way, other Africans from other villages were also being captured, some with different languages and cultures. Before being hoarded onto ships, the unsuspecting villagers were beaten along the way, and for those who resisted, their lives ended in death. The point of no return stood as ominous forts where villagers were packed in along these cold, stone walls and dirt floors, wet with the stench of seeping body fluids from hundreds of men, women and children. The stench was overpowering, and nothing could be done to rewind this nightmare. The story is a well-known one to all of us now, but the pain in the memory of such a torturous time is impossible to erase. Despite their unimaginable torture, these Africans were able to maintain much of their own inner music, their cultural beliefs and folklore, and in their manner and methods of cooking. Out of this painful passage grew a unique culture of people and within this culture grew many slices of ingenuity and talent that cannot be replicated. Slave and free African Americans were often highly skilled in their homelands and were, therefore, often selected specifically because of those special skills needed to enhance growth and productivity in the new world – America. Many African American lives were simply forgotten and not honored for their lives and contributions to the new world. However, to honor the memory of those many unknowns, **The Tomb of the Unknown Slave** was created in New Orleans, LA at St. Augustine Catholic Church. The memorial is made with giant chains hung with shackles.

Before being sold into slavery, these stolen Africans were people with independence, skills, pride and artful talents of all kinds, including carpentry, farming, and cooking. They lived mostly from the fruits and vegetables grown on their lands. The introduction of a fat filled diet came from European influences that surrounded them after arrival in the Americas as slaves. Many of the Africans that were transported against their will from their native African shores were of the Muslim faith and did not eat pork or animals that were considered unclean. However, food choices for slaves were often very limited. Slave masters fed their slaves portions of animals that would normally be thrown away or fed to other animals (i.e. chitterlings, neck bones, chicken feet, pig feet, pig snout, etc.) Foods in the American south came to be known as the 3M's (meat, meal, and molasses), all which later became unhealthy food choices for the previously healthy Africans. Pork was highly valued by southern plantation owners, and then it became a slave staple. Two hundred years ago upon arrival from Africa, boiling greens over the hearth fire, became one of America's most comforting cuisines, cooked by Africans across the continent.

Diets of slaves would vary based on work assignment and social interactions. House slaves ate foods more akin to their slave owners, while field slaves ate entrails and other foods that were thrown away. To supplement their diets, many field slaves would dig roots from the ground, pick berries and other fruit from trees or vines, or fish to help them survive – anything that would keep their families strong and better fed. Research has documented the longevity of the lives of many African slaves, some well into their eighties and nineties, despite the hardships of their living conditions.[3] One study conducted at Stanford University Medical School on Ethnogeriatrics concludes: *"There may have developed within the "slave community" means of self health care that helped young and old slaves to withstand the hazards of everyday life during the antebellum period".* I contend that what my ancestors transformed into "Soul Food" developed from a need to preserve the "slave community" and the state of the physical and mental health of those growing up in that community. It became an unwritten responsibility in the African American community, then and even now, to nurture the soul through what one creates for the body's nourishment. In doing so, African Americans helped to save an entire race of people. During her 19 journeys to transports slaves from bondage in the south to freedom in the north, Sojourner Truth provided roasted potatoes,, fish, fruits and vegetables to sustain these slaves on this dangerous and treacherous trip. They would move 10 – 20 miles a day, mostly on foot, to reach the next eat station. She was someone who nurtured, nourished and encouraged those who would be the foundation for the next free generation of African Americans. In our culture, those elders who are gifted with wisdom, passed from one generation to the next, are the most respected in our families and they are held in high esteem in our families. They are repositories for our stories, our songs, our recipes, our secrets. All this wisdom and knowledge has become the embodiment of what Soul Food really is. It should not be thought of as merely that which has fed our bellies, but a bonding agent that continues to bring us together in celebration of all that we have accomplished and overcome.

---

[3] https://geriatrics.stanford.edu/ethnomed/african_american/fund/health_history/longevity.html

GIFTS OF THE GULLAH CULTURE

The Gullah people were descendants of Africans who were thought to be from the area of Angola in Africa. These descendants blended with others from other coastal areas of Africa – all who were brought into the "low country" of South Carolina near the city of Charleston, a primary port during the height of slave trading. Many soul foods are directly accredited to the Gullah people and their ancestral cooking methods. These foods include peanuts, okra, rice, yams, peas, bennie seeds, hot peppers, sorghum and watermelon. Gullah people are sometimes referred to as Geechee. The name Gullah came to be associated with West African slave descendants who settled along the South Carolina coast. The name **Geechee** refers to who settled along the Georgia coast. Both have kept the African cultural traditions since the mid-1700s. These coastal island slaves were specifically sought out from the areas near Angola or Sierre Leon because of their expertise in growing rice and creating indigo. They also brought with them the knowledge for harvesting rice using the wheat grass fanner baskets that aided in winnowing the rice (method of separating the grain from the chaff).

CREOLE CULTURE FOOD CONTRIBUTIONS

The term Creole is used to distinguish the difference between people born in Louisiana (originally a French settlement) from those Frenchmen from the mother country (France). These people were usually of mixed race. The Creoles spoke French and strongly connected themselves to the French colonial culture. The language and cooking of the Creole people, however is a unique combination of the African, Native American, French and Spanish cultures.

A Creole meal is considered a celebration. Those dishes that have an African influence from Creoles of color include shrimp, crab, varieties of fish, gumbos, stews (enhanced with experimental combination of spices) and sassafras roots and leaves. Foods in this region include Crayfish, crab, oysters, shrimp and salt-water fish.

AFRICAN AMERICAN HISTORY IN SEAFOOD

Seafood Spaghetti

Seafood became a staple of Africans bought to the Americas in bondage and to those who lived as free African Americans in the north. African Americans found ways to supplement their family diets. Following the emancipation of all slaves in 1864, most freed Blacks worked in the fields, doing the same things that they had done when they were enslaved. Because job opportunities were limited due to discrimination, many African Americans turned to the seafood industry as a way of earning a living and feeding their families. In 1864, 40% of all watermen on the **Chesapeake Bay in Maryland** were ex-slaves. They would work from dawn to dusk and would nearly freeze in the winters. It was extremely hard work being a waterman. However, they became very proficient in fishing, harvesting oysters, netting shrimp, and learning about the seafood industry overall. Seafood, therefore, became a primary food staple in African American families along coastal areas from Maryland to Florida and in the Caribbean as African Americans created a means for supporting themselves. Many even created a livelihood from the seafood industry.

LOW COUNTRY CUISINE

Foods in the "Low Country' region (Carolinas, Virginia & Georgia) include fish, shrimp, oysters which were and still are often mixed with rice and okra. This seafood is very similar to Creole and Cajun cuisines. Rice is one of the primary staples in this region. West Africans introduced the rice plant and its cultivation to North America. West Africans had grown the rice plant since 100 A.D.

The subtropical climate has had a great influence on the cooking in the "low country" region. Methods for preserving food were important. An abundance of fruits like peaches and berries enhanced the flavors of prepared dishes. They were pickled, stewed and used in a variety of ways to enhance meals for the families. Figs, brought to the region by the Spaniards became a "low country" favorite, used as a condiment or a preserve. According to author Martin Taylor, a native of this region, food prepared in this region is a comfort food, centered around one-pot dishes of stews, seafood boils, grits, and many other dish combinations, all with flavors from across the globe.

NATIVE AMERICAN, LATIN, & CARIBBEAN INFLUENCES ON SOUL FOOD CUISINE

BLACK NATIVE AMERICAN INDIAN

NATIVE AMERICAN FOOD WAYS - The relationship between the American Indian and African American has been a very complex one. The first record of connection between these two very different cultures was reported to have begun in 1502 when enslaved Africans were taken to Hispaniola but then escaped to San Antonio. What emerged was the first mixing of these two races of people – the first Black Native.[4] Because some Native Americans also owned slaves in the south, the relationship with African Americans remained a rocky one through the end of the Civil War. Some Africans escaped to Florida, became a part of the Seminole Tribe, and traveled with them when forced to move across the country to government created Native American territories. The very sad saga of the **"Trail of Tears"** recounts the horrid reality suffered by not only the Native American Cherokee Tribe, but also the African Americans that traveled with them as slaves. One Cherokee man, Nathaniel Willis, remembered that in the 1930s - ***"My grandparents were helped and protected by***

---

[4] EBONY MAGAZINE article 5 Things to Know About Blacks and Native Americans, November 20, 2012 by Team Ebony

very faithful Negro slaves who . . . went ahead of the wagons and killed any wild beast that came along". [5]

Both Native Americans and African Americans died of starvation or effects of very bitter winters as they were forced to leave their native land – land that was then stolen by Whites who removed them from their homes and land. The blending of these two cultures also lent itself to the blending of their foodways. African Americans from the coastal areas of North and South America who escaped to Florida found safe haven with the Seminole Indians. They taught these Native Americans rice cultivation and the Indians shared with them the many uses of corn, squash and hominy that became staples in the African American diet.

"To a far greater degree than anyone realizes, several of the most important food dishes of the Southeastern Indians live on today in the "soul food" eaten by both black and white Southerners. **Hominy**, *for example, is still eaten ... Sofkee live on as* **grits** *... * **cornbread** *[is] used by Southern cooks ... Indian fritters ... variously known as* **"hoe cake",** *... or "Johnny cake". ... Indians boiled cornbread is present in Southern cuisine as* **"corn meal dumplings",** *... and as* **"hush puppies",** *... Southern cook their beans and field peas by boiling them, as did the Indians ... like the Indians they cure their meat and smoke it over hickory coals."*—- Charles Hudson, The Southeastern Indians"[6]

One of my favorite food memories, from my home in Oklahoma, had its root from the Native American community. *Indian Fry Bread*, according to Navajo history, was created circa 1864; over time, this food for the soul became a staple on the tables of African Americans as well.

---

[5] CNN – In America – Painful Trail of Tears Shared by Black as Well As Native Americans, 2-25-1-2012 http://inamerica.blogs.cnn.com/2012/02/25/pain-of-trail-of-tears-shared-by-blacks-as-well-as-native-americans/ Posted by Cameo George - CNN

[6] Hudsen, Charles (1976). "A Conquered People". *The Southeastern Indians*. University of Tennessee Press. pp. 498–499. ISBN 0-87049-248-

PUERTO RICAN CUISINE

LATINO FOODWAYS – African American and Latino foods formed an alliance that grew out of the migrations of diverse people from the Americas, Europe, Africa, and Asia. Their history has been shaped by the common experience that spread widely across the American continent as their various cultures intermingled. One of the most common foods shared by both African Americans and Latinos is beans and rice, cooked in many different varieties and combinations. The feeding of cow intestines to slaves began in European countries, beginning with those of Spanish descent.

CARIBBEAN CUISINE - Dishes such as ***ambalaya* (mixed rice, meat and vegetables)**; ***feijoada* (black beans and meat)**, ***gombo* (okra)**, and ***hopping john* (peas)** are all dishes that have been re-adapted from Senegal, Nigeria, Guinea and Benin. Variations of these African dishes found their way up and down the American southern coast and into the Caribbean. The ***sauces feuilles* or "sauce from vegetable leaves"** from Guinée is also found in Haiti and Jamaica in other variations.

African slaves brought to Caribbean shores combined their African knowledge of cooking and the spices and fruits found in that region and created a unique diet that gave birth to cooking methods such a **"jerk"** (cooking without smoke to keep their hideouts a secret). With the arrival of Indian and Chinese laborers to the Caribbean Islands in the 19th century, the spice curry and mustard were added to the island cuisine.

METAMORPHESIS OF THE AMERICAN CULINARY PALATE

As centuries passed, there was a metamorphosis in the way slaves cooked and ate. Africans from the coastal region near Ghana, Benin and Nigeria shared a diet of root crops like yams and vegetable stews seasoned with a variety of spicy sauces. Those shipped to the Americas from the regions closer to Middle Africa during the Middle Passage[7] shared diets that included millet, honey, palm oil, plantains, potatoes, coca nuts, casaba, limes, grapes, cinnamon and rice. Slaves assigned to cook for their masters continued cooking in the manner they were used to in Africa, but integrated animal fats and local American spices to enhance the flavors of these new and unfamiliar European foodstuffs. The lines between what was purely African and purely European became very blurred over time. Creative cooks, with these culinary blends and artful manipulations of starches, spices, fats, and fruits, transformed just ordinary meals into what became southern delicacies over many decades. This method of cooking came to be known as "Soul Food" between the 1950s – 1960s. The term 'soul' attached itself to the food creations of the descendants of creative slave cooks because it evoked a deeply soulful emotion in both African Americans and White Americans. White Americans, however, called their new way of eating "Southern Cuisine".

The transition of the way in which southern foods were prepared by slaves was often dictated by the region in which they lived and how foods were preserved. In the article "The Real Roots of Southern Cuisine" [8]written by Atlanta Chef Todd Richards, he writes:

TR: "To me, greens tell the unique story of Southern food. There was no refrigeration, so slaves used meat, mostly pork, and salt to preserve the greens by laying the meat on top. Not only did the pork preserve what was underneath, but it flavored it as well. They didn't necessarily eat the meat after the greens were finished. They might repurpose it. Frying was another technique. Many people are shocked to learn that fried chicken is not Southern-born but Scandinavian and Native American. Animals in West Africa were not fatty. It was hot; they didn't need fat to stay warm. Frying was a preservation method the slaves adopted."

In the book "Soul Food Love" written by sisters Alice Randall and Caroline Randall Williams, these authors share family stories built around the love of soul food covering five generations of their ancestors. Their book explores the often-fraught relationship African-American women have had with food, and forges a powerful new way forward that honors their cultural and culinary heritage. According to these chefs, the soul food diet has been known to cause health problems

---

[7] Middle Passage – The stage of the triangular trade when millions of Africans were shipped to America
[8] The Real Roots of Southern Cuisine, DEEP SOUTH Magazine, December 3, 2012.

because of its overabundant use of fat, starchy food and sugar. Modern chefs have tried to reverse the effects of this traditional method of cooking, moving more towards vegan dishes, but vegan with a soulful edge. However, the heart of soul food has never been just the food; its soulfulness includes the love, patience, creativity and bonding formed from passing down family recipes and traditions from generation to generation of African American families.

In the National Geographic article "How Slaves Shaped American Cooking" by Karen Pinchin, researched slaves' stories chronicle the transformation of African cooking methods into the daily fabric of American life. One of the stories in part is a wonderful example:

David Shields, a professor at the University of South Carolina in Columbia and an expert in early American literature and food revivals, points to Emeline Jones as an example.

Jones was a slave who started as a house servant and rose to the pinnacle of American culinary life with her extravagant multicourse meals. She earned admiration—and job offers—from Presidents Garfield, Arthur, and Cleveland, who sampled her fabulous meals of terrapin and canvasback duck, Lynnhaven oysters and crab salad, hominy cakes and fabulous confections, prepared when Jones worked as a cook at New York clubs in the late 1870s.

Another story, from the 1937 U.S. government Work Projects Administration under the reign of President Roosevelt, a slave narrative from "***The Hairston Story** – Georgia Plantation Slave Food Ration*" gives a bird's eye view of the daily rations consumed by slaves, from the actual word of a former slave:

"Potlicker and cornbread was fed to us chillun, out of big old wooden bowls. Two or three chillun et out of de same bowl. Grown folks had meat, greens, syrup, cornbread, 'taters and de lak. 'Possums! I should say so. Dey cotch plenty of 'em and atter dey was kilt ma would scald 'em and rub 'em in hot ashes and dat clean't 'em jus' as pretty and white.

OO-o-o but dey was good. Lord, Yessum! Dey used to go fishin' and rabbit huntin' too. Us jus' fotched in game galore den, for it was de style dem days. Dere warn't no market meat in slavery days. Seemed lak to me in dem days dat ash-roasted 'taters and ground peas was de best somepin t'eat what anybody could want. 'Course dey had a gyarden, and it had somepin of jus' about evvything what us knowed anything 'bout in de way of gyarden sass growin' in it. All de cookin' was done in dem big old open fireplaces what was fixed up special for de pots and ovens. Ashcake was most as good as 'taters cooked in de ashes, but not quite.

In the Book, "When I was a Slave", slave Fannie Moore describes methods of canning and preserving food seasonally:

"De way dey done, dey peel de peaches and cut 'em up. Den dey put layer of peaches ina crock, den a layer of sugar, den a layer of peaches until de crock was full. Den dey seal de jar by puttin' a cloth over the top, then a layer of paste, then another cloth, then another layer of paste. Dey can most of de other fruit and put it in de same kind of jars dat de peaches in."

"Folks back den never hear tell of all de ailments de folks have now...Just use roots and bark for teas of all kinds."

SOUL FOODS KNOWN BY OTHER NAMES FROM OTHER PLACES

As foods from our African roots transformed over and over again, they came to be known by many different names. Author Jocelyne Sambria mentions many of these food transformations in an on-line article in the AfricaRenewal blog *"Slave trade: How African foods influenced modern American Cuisine".*

Rice pudding became a culinary treat in the Carolinas and in the Caribbean. But its origin is from Senegal. Slave traders sought out specific regions in Africa where rice was cultivated. Casmance, a region in the South of Senegal was one of those areas. This rice became known as **"Carolina Gold"**.

A dish called **Akaraje**, well known in Brazil, was first known in West Africa. There it was known as Akara – a dish made from black-eyed peas. When mashed into a grainy form it was used in the New Orleans regions to make beignets.

"Hopping John" (peas & rice), a dish popular in the Carolinas is one that was readopted from the Senegalese area of Africa, also known as feijoada (black beans and meat). New Orleans residents created their own unique version of this transformative dish and called it **Jambalaya (mixed rice, meat and vegetables.)**

Okra, another vegetable that originated in Africa became the primary base for the popular dish **"gumbo"**. This manner of cooking was an adaptation of **"soupikandia", a Senegalese soupy stew.**

Citrullus lanatus is the African ancestor of what we know as **watermelon**. It was originally grown in the arid regions of Africa because of its ability to store moisture. Research shows this fruit to have been a staple of ancient Egyptians – found in tombs of Egyptians Pharaohs.

Black-eyed peas originated in Southern and Central Africa, known as **vigna unguiculata**. It is a high protein legume brought over on slave ships as a provision for the slaves. It was also used to feed cattle, therefore becoming also known as "cowpeas". It is still a popular staple in the soul food diet.

Coffee, typically associated with the South American region, was grown in Ethiopia, known as **coffea Arabica**. Ethiopia is recognized as the birthplace coffee.

THE SOUL FOOD MUSEUM JOURNEY CONTINUES

I now continue my journey that I started over 40 years ago, first collecting in my home, then moving it to **Big Bethel Church in Atlanta**, then to a building in Atlanta on historic Auburn Avenue. Following my struggle through a harsh economic downturn, I kept my historic soul food collection alive as a mobile unit. I had to keep my dream alive of telling the soul food story in my own way. As a chef, I proudly share what I consider a very important part of the African American story – my story, and the story of all African American descendants of slaves brought to this country beginning in 1619.

My story is a visual story, manifested through the many items that I have collected. My collections range from African American collectible images of Aunt Jemima and Uncle Ben to Famous Amos Cookies, commercial business successes, racially offensive images that bring back painful memories of segregation, replicas of African American inventions, and endless other familiar and sometimes rare items worth noting as part of our soul food and hospitality industry story.

As my journey to educate the world about the history of the soul food continues, I share my collection in words and images via this virtual tour through my Soul Food Museum/book of knowledge that I trust will take this story around the world.

So, my virtual tour through the Soul Food Museum begins. This page-by-page tour is one that you can return to over and over again and share with family, friends and others for generations to come. As you "walk" through my museum with me, I hope that you will garner an understanding of my struggle and that of my ancestors for over 400 years. Despite our struggles, we have left a legacy of unbreakable spirits, continuously evolving to make the world that we all live in a better place.

IMPORTANCE OF TELLING AND RETELLING OUR STORIES

My ancestors, the slaves that were brought to this land against their will, did one thing that ultimately became an extraordinary gift to me. Unknowingly, they became Griots for the generations to come, and I am one of those fortunate recipients. My ancestors couldn't read and couldn't write, but they could remember, and remember they did. Slave narratives I have read give vivid directions about how family's favorite dishes should be cooked, how and when to plant certain vegetables, and exactly what seasonings should be used to make an ordinary dish, one of almost magical proportions.

My love of food is not an accident. It was planted deep in me, not just by my grandmother, but also by my grandmother's mother who taught her. That generational seedling grew into not only a chef, but also another generation's Griot. Telling and retelling our stories is akin to passing a baton in a relay race, and that race will be one that is continuous and endless – from one generation to the next. We must pass that baton with deliberate precision. The lessons we have learned must be passed on to those who come behind us. My great, great grandmother took the hand of her young children and showed them how to plant those seeds that grew into plants that would then nourish them. My great grandmother showed us how to raise chickens and collect their eggs. Then she showed us how ring their necks and how to pluck their feathers, so our bellies wouldn't be empty when times were hard. We learned, by watching their struggle, that there was always a way through the storm.

My grandmother used to sit us all in the middle of the kitchen in a circle when there was real storm outside. She would make us sit quietly and just listen to the voice of God. She told us that the powerful boom we heard in the storm was God talking. We sat in silence, just listening. And before we knew it, the storm was over. African Americans stories are like that relay race, but only this race has continuously been in the midst of a storm. When the storm clouds cleared, it was again time to get back to work and then tell others how we survived the storm because we know that other storms will surely come.

During slavery, it was illegal for Black people to read because knowledge is power, and those holding the power do not want those they wish to control to have the same power that they have. However, knowledge comes not only from reading. Knowledge comes also from hearing the words of those who came before us, listening intently, and regurgitating those lessons into action. So, during and even many years after slavery, it was imperative that elders talk to their 'younguns'. Once African Americans began to learn to read, then their lessons were passed on in their letters, in their journals, and ultimately in their own books, newspapers, on film, in plays, as teachers and more.

It is now my responsibility to pass on my ancestors' baton – by example, in my words, in my work as a Culinary Historian, and by sharing my collection of African American culinary artifacts in this Soul Food Museum.

So, I now pass the baton as it was passed to me to educate, to uplift, to inspire, and to prepare those that come behind me for their storms.

THE BLACK STATUE OF LIBERTY HISTORICAL REFERENCE

The image of the Soul Food Museum Lady Liberty was my vision that I created in 2002. It was inspired by the statue that was presented to the United States in 1886 by the French government. The original statue was an image of a Black woman included a view of broken shackles (noted in the book titled "Journey of the Sangii People" authored by Jim Haskins). This original statue was rejected by the United States and the statue that stands today in the New York Harbor as the "Statue of Liberty" continues to greet immigrants as they strive to begin their lives in this new country.

In searching for a logo for the National African American Culinary Arts & Hospitality Association, I created an image formed from my love and respect for five beautiful and powerful women who are shining examples of the best of our culture. In my logo are embedded features from each of these women: Aretha Franklin, Maya Angelou, Gladys Knight, Oprah Winfrey, and Pattie LaBelle.

THE TOUR ...

*The History, The Struggle, The Survival, and
The Contributions*

**Educating the World on the History of Soul Food,
Hospitality, Service & Agriculture**

VIRTUAL TOUR
THROUGH MY SOUL FOOD MUSEUM...

EXHIBIT 1

CELEBRATION OF THE HUMAN SPIRIT
– SOUL FOOD TRADITIONS

When one generally thinks of soul food traditions, one thinks of a Thanksgiving family table covered from one end to the other with fried chicken, ham, biscuits, yams, macaroni and cheese, and of course, collard greens. A soul food feast wouldn't be complete without the collard greens. Family feasts of this sort were, however, not limited to just a once a year holiday gathering. In some families, soul food feasts happened every Sunday after church, or every time grandma came to visit. It could be every time relatives came into town for a visit or each time there was a graduation, baby shower, wedding and even the repast after a funeral.

It was not until after the emancipation of slaves, that African American families were able to come together comfortably in celebration and unity. These gatherings, centered around foods that warmed the soul and lifted the spirit, were a celebration of the family unit that had, for over centuries, been torn apart at the whim and will of the white masters. The plantation masters used the power of 'divide and conquer' to control slaves. When freedom finally came, African Americans looked for every opportunity to feast. The gathering of family around the table became a feast of survival, a feast of togetherness, a feast of love.

Different families created their unique traditions surrounding these feasts. In some families the cooking began a week in advance, with rituals of shelling peas and picking ends off of the fresh green beans bunched together on crisp white aprons covering the laps of Auntie and Sister. The kitchen was filled with the freshness of vegetables just picked from the garden, and with raucous laughter and chatter, the whole time the meal was being prepared. There would be the elders and the younguns all hovered together in the kitchen, each with their own task to complete for the big feast. One could almost identify the creator of certain dishes instantly because of the special kind of magic specific cooks would add to their specialty and the pride they showed in identifying which was their creation. It would even become a bit competitive at times – a source of sensitivity as new wives or other relatives were added to the family. Traditionally, at a New Year's Eve feast there must be collard greens to ensure that the family wouldn't be broke in the New Year, and black-eyed peas are still a must to bring in the New Year with good luck. Whatever the tradition, the act of preparing, the joy of coming together in preparation of the meal, and then eating it, allowed families to still be grounded and connected. These traditions of gathering for food feasts have waned somewhat as families began to migrate to other parts of the country and began to spend more time working than communing with family. The Soul Food feast is a dying celebration that seems to have played a significant role in the disintegration of the African American family, as we once knew it.

In an interview by Kristin Boyd in the Reading Eagle, down-home cook Maeola Ellison explained the soul food tradition in her family this way:

> *Black folks just enjoy eating together", the Reading resident said with a laugh. "I don't know why we do. We like the family being together.*
>
> *"All the kids would come over for Sunday dinner or family dinner, and we would cook and talk. It's how we stayed close."*
>
> *In the past, weekly Sunday dinners were a requirement, not a choice. Typically served after church, they provided best family time to bond, eat, share stories, recount memories and just laugh till your stomach hurt.*

---

[9]No other event could have facilitated such education. The large family dinners of my youth had been replaced by occasional, smaller, single-family gatherings or feasts at banquet style restaurants. But at this gathering, under the charismatic authority of our elders, history that had been silenced for far too long, was given voice and form and enlisted to mobilize generations of unasked questions. The significance of this opportunity for my family (and for other families) is pivotal in the preservation of African American culture as elders step forward to teach and be taught, strengthen and be strengthened.

---

[9] GENERATIONS – African American Elders, Cultural Traditions and the Family Reunion, Posted 11-18-2011

EXHIBIT 2

SLAVES DAY OFF

It seems hard to imagine, but on most plantations in southern America and the Caribbean, slavery was slavery, but even slaves had a day off. That day was Sunday when the plantation masters spent the day in church and communing with family. Slaves used that day in a more enterprising manner – tending to their personal gardens or trading the fruits and vegetables from their personal labors in the marketplace.[10] They grew sweet potatoes, yams, vegetables and plantains in the Caribbean, which they would sell or use to supplement their own diets. From the 17th century onward, it became customary for plantation owners to give their slaves the day off.

Image - *Sunday Morning in the Country'; enslaved Africans going to market in Trinidad. Source Richard Bridgens, West India Scenery... from sketches taken during a voyage to, and residence of seven years in... Trinidad (London, 1836), plate 15)*

---

[10] Diet and Food Production for Enslaved Africans, International Slavery Market

EXHIBIT 3

SOUL FOOD FOLKLORE

Surrounding the joy of cooking and eating soul food are also generations of folklore passed down from one ancestor to the next. Each food source generated a lore, spell or song of its own, becoming more embellished with time. Here are just a few memorable ones:

- According to folklore, collards served with black-eyed peas and hog jowl on New Year's Day promises a year of luck and financial prosperity. Hanging a fresh leaf over your door will ward off evil spirits. And a fresh leaf placed on your forehead promises to cure a headache. Black-eyed peas were not just black-eyed peas. They were put on people's graves, thrown into paths for good luck to make women fertile. Each food had its proverbs, songs, spells, and lore.
- Stories passed on over the years reveal that the black-eyed peas are supposed to resemble coins. The greens are supposed to represent the dollar bills and the cornbread is supposed to represent the gold. It is said that by eating them, they are supposed to bring you prosperity for the new year.

- [11][12]The expression ***"high on the hog"*** refers to the choice cuts of pork, those from the loin, shoulder and upper leg, long reserved for the elite. The ***"low on the hog"*** cuts like belly, trotters and offal were left for poor folk. So naturally, pork, with its rich, delicious fattiness has come to symbolize wealth and prosperity. With so many options such as sausage, ribs, bacon, ham, suckling pig, etc. there's no reason not to be in ***"hog heaven"*** for at least one day.

- Cowpeas aka Black–eyed peas, also known as field peas, were used to feed grazing cattle. During the Siege of Vicksburg, Mississippi in the late spring of 1863, the town was cut off from all food supplies for nearly two months. The people were close to starvation and resorted to eating the crops previously reserved for feeding their livestock. It has been said that if it weren't for the lowly "cowpeas" many people wouldn't have survived.

- Greens - greenbacks...moola? Makes sense. Leafy greens resemble folded paper money symbolizing wealth and prosperity. Pair them with black–eyed peas and ham for a truly Southern New Year's tradition (both high on the luck spectrum) and triple your luck for the year.

- **Gospel Bird** - Eatin' the "gospel bird" (Fried Chicken) was a reference to the presence of preachers at family dining room tables after church on Sundays, especially when fried chicken was being served.

- **Nashville Spicy Chicken** – One popular folklore story that grew out of Prince's Hot Chicken Shack in Nashville, Tennessee claims that spicy chicken became popular based on the reputation of its owner as a womanizer. That owner and cook was Thornton Prince. According to the story passed down since the 1930s, Prince's lady friend, suspecting him of infidelity, served him up his favorite dish – fried chicken – but she added peppers and hot spices to get back at Prince. However, her plan backfired because he loved the new chicken creation. Her creation then inspired Prince to open his now famous Hot Chicken Shack that is still in business to this day.[13]

---

[11] http://www.phrases.org.uk/meanings/high-on-the-hog.html

[12] First We Feast – 15 Delicious Things That Were Created by Mistake. http://firstwefeast.com/eat/2013/09/foods-invented-mistake/nashville-hot-chicken

[13] Erica Taylor, Little Known Black History Facts – The Tom Joyner Morning Show
https://blackamericaweb.com/2013/03/28/little-known-black-history-fact-the-history-of-aunt-jemima/

EXHIBIT 4

AFRICAN AMERICAN FOOD INDUSTRY INVENTORS AND AGRICULTURAL INNOVATORS

Henry Blair

Born in 1807, Blair was a farmer and the second African-American to be granted a patent. He was also the first to invent two devices to boost farm productivity: a seed planter and a cotton planter. Blair accomplished all of this despite being illiterate. His patents were challenged in court by a slave-owner, though Blair was never enslaved.

George Washington Carver 1864 - 1943

Contrary to popular belief, Carver did not invent peanut butter. A botanist and inventor, he published a research bulletin called "How to Grow the Peanut and 105 Ways of Preparing it for Human Consumption" in 1916. The document includes interesting ways to use peanuts, including in items like shampoo, mayonnaise, and paints. He also advised Indian leader Mahatma Gandhi on matters of agriculture and nutrition. Dr. George Washington Carver invented over 300 products using the peanut and over 100 products from sweet potatoes.

Lloyd Augustus Hall 1894 -1971

Hall was a chemist who contributed to the science of food preservation. His research led to improved curing salts and meat preservation. He also discovered a method for sterilizing spices for the meat packing industry that preserved food without loss of appearance, quality or flavor. During his career, he amassed 59 patents. His method of curing meat is still in use today.

———————————————————————————————

Percy Julian 1899 – 1975

As a research chemist, Julian was a pioneer in the chemical synthesis of medicinal drugs from plants. His research helped trigger an explosive growth industry for soybeans and uncovered new uses for the chemicals found in soybeans. For example, a protein he extracted from soybeans was used to produce a fire-retardant foam in fire extinguishers, which saved thousands of soldiers' lives during World War II.

———————————————————————————————

Joseph Lee 1849 -1919

Lee grew up working in a bakery and as an adult opened two successful restaurants. As a business owner, he was interested in limiting the amount of wasted bread, which would be thrown out if it was more than one day old. To fix this problem, Lee invented a device that could mechanize tearing, crumbling, and grinding bread into crumbs.

Benjamin Banneker 1849 -1919

Banneker created the first American clock after taking apart and studying a pocket watch that he borrowed from someone. This was 1750. With much study and research, Banneker also created the farmer's almanac. He was selected by Thomas Jefferson to be a part of the surveying team that laid out the plans for Washington, D.C. He is recognized in history as a scientist, inventor, and anti-slavery proponent.

Norbert Rillieux 1806 – 1894

Rillieux is most well-known for his invention of the multiple-effect evaporator, an energy-efficient means of evaporating water. The invention was an important development in the growth of the sugar industry. Rillieux was recognized as one of America's early chemical engineers. By 1848 Rillieux's system was successfully producing finer, whiter sugar with a huge reduction in costs and labor.

McKinley Jones (1893-1961) - An orphan with a sixth-grade education, gave the world its first refrigerated truck. This gave grocery stores and other companies the ability to transport food long distances without it spoiling. This was a dramatic change from using ice – which was unreliable. With his invention, the world changed the way it transported food.

Alexander P. Ashbourne

On November 30, 1875, **Alexander P. Ashbourne** invented a biscuit cutter. Ashbourne (c.1820-1915) was an African American grocery store owner in Oakland, California.

EXHIBIT 5

AFRICAN AMERICAN FOOD CREATIONS

Marshmallow candy was first made by ancient Egyptians over three thousand years ago. The Egyptians made candy from the root of the **marshmallow plant** (***Althea officinalis***), a plant that grows in marshes. Today's marshmallows do not have any mallow root - gelatin is substituted for the sweet, sticky root.

POTATO CHIPS

The potato chip was invented in **1853** by ***George Crum***. Crum was a Native American/ African American chef at the Moon Lake Lodge resort in Saratoga Springs, New York, USA. French fries were popular at the restaurant and one day a diner complained that the fries were too thick. Although Crum made a thinner batch, the customer was still unsatisfied. Crum finally made fries that were too thin to eat with a fork, hoping to annoy the extremely fussy customer. The customer, surprisingly enough, was happy - and potato chips were invented!

Because Mr. Crumb did not patent his creation, others went on to make billions of dollars from his original idea, beginning with William Tappendon, the first to mass market the potato chip. http://www.enchantedlearning.com/inventors/food.shtml.

———————————————————————————

AFRICAN AMERICAN FOODS AND FLAVORS

Over many decades, there has been a blend of European and foods of African roots. However, certain foods and flavors continue to be identified as those used primarily in African American soul food dishes.

FLAVORS – Brown Sugar
Cayenne Pepper
Cornmeal (staple of African American slaves)
Salt Pork
Paprika
Nutmeg
Hot Peppers
Garlic
Sesame Seed

FOODS - Coffee
Black-Eyed Peas, Kidney Beans, Pigeon Peas
Okra (Brought from Africa with slaves), Cucumber, Spinach, Onion
Yams (African plant different from Sweet Potatoes brought to America in the late 1400s)
Peanuts (Brought from Africa with slaves – African name for **peanut** is
nguba, which later became "goober" in southern American)
Dates, Figs, Oranges, Watermelon
Eggplant, Squash, Pumpkin, Squash, Rice, Collard Greens

EXHIBIT 6

MEMORABILIA & MEMORABLE PLACES

AUNT JEMIMA

In 1890, a former slave named Nancy Green was hired to be the spokesperson for **Aunt Jemima** brand food products. Nancy Green was born into slavery in 1834 in Montgomery County, Kentucky. In 1889 the creators of Aunt Jemima, the recognizable image for pancake mix, Charles Rutt and Charles Underwood, sold the company to R.T Davis, who soon found Nancy Green in Chicago. The previous owners had already agreed upon her 'look' of a bandana and an apron. Davis combined the Aunt Jemima look with a catchy tune from the Vaudeville circuit to make the Aunt Jemima brand. [14]

The original **"Uncle Ben"** was a rice farmer, famous for the quality of his crop. His commitment to producing only the best rice inspired the company to market this product by using his name in their advertising efforts. That reflects the passion for the products that the company makes.

---

[14] https://afroculinaria.com/2015/02/19/soul-foodies-to-watch-charla-draper

Chicken Bone Beach was a racially segregated section of the Atlantic Ocean beach at Atlantic City, New Jersey known for attracting many African American families and entertainers. The nickname, Chicken Bone Beach, derived affectionately from the tradition of the thousands of vacationing families who flocked to the shore bringing beach balls, umbrellas and blankets for ocean-side fun and picnic baskets with fried chicken and other delights for seaside dining. When they finished eating, they buried the chicken bones in the sand.

http://www.blackpast.org/aah/chicken-bone-beach-atlantic-city-new-jersey.

––––––––––––––––––––––––––––––––––––––

African Americans opposed this blatant display of racial hostility. In 1930, the Seattle branch of the National Association for the Advancement for Colored People (NAACP) and Seattle's African American newspaper, The Northwest Enterprise, protested the opening of the local **Coon Chicken Inn** by threatening Graham with a lawsuit for libel and defamation of race. In response, Graham agreed to change the style of advertising by removing the word 'Coon' from the restaurant's delivery car, repainting the 'Coon head' entrance to the restaurant, and canceling an order of 1,000 automobile tire covers. This small stride, however, was not enough to fully erase the image of the caricature from Seattle. Graham violated his agreement with the NAACP but managed to evade the lawsuit by changing the color of the Coon logo from black to blue. Graham closed the Seattle and Portland locations in 1949. The Coon Chicken Inn restaurant in Salt Lake City, however, stayed open until 1957. ***http://www.blackpast.org/aaw/coon-chicken-inn#sthash.ktv7QvVP.dpuf.***

From 1926 – 1974 beach areas along the Chesapeake Bay and Atlantic Ocean coast designated solely for African Americans during this period of segregation in America.

––––––––––––––––––––––––––––––––––––––

After reconstruction, it was an uphill struggle for African Americans to find their place in an American that was still so unaccepting. Many Europeans felt that African Americans were still less than human despite the reality that people (no matter their color) are just people. The 14th Amendment constitutional change of 1868 made this reality a legal matter when it became law.

With the help of the Hotel Trades Council, the hotel union signed an agreement in the early 1930s that affected 20,000 African Americans, as they became a part of the hospitality industry as hotel waiters, bellman and maid's union. This significant inroad meant that African Americans now received equal wages and work hours as all other union members in certain parts of the country.

This landmark event occurred in New York City, New York. It would be many, many years before equality in the hospitality and food service industry would be inclusive of all people, including people of all colors and ethnicities across our entire country.

EXHIBIT 7

RECOMMENDED READING

HOGS & HOMINY   **Author – Frederick Douglas Opie**

Frederick Douglass Opie deconstructs and compares the foodways of people of African descent throughout the Americas, interprets the health legacies of black culinary traditions, and explains the concept of soul itself. His book reveals soul food to be a blend of West and Central African social and cultural influences as well as the adaptations Blacks made to the conditions of slavery and freedom in the Americas.

HOW TO EAT TO LIVE   **Author - Minister Elijah Muhammad**

Series of two books published in the 1960s, which discusses the philosophy of Minister Elijah Muhammad about healthy living and the diet of Black Muslims.

SOUL VEGETARIAN   **From the Kitchens of Soul Vegetarian Restaurant**

With several restaurant locations dotted across the United States, Soul Vegetarian Restaurants have offered healthy cuisine to its communities for over 25 years. Their cookbooks offer a cross-section of the restaurant's favorite foods that are 100% plant based --- animal and chemical free.

SOUL FOOD – The Surprising Story of An American Cuisine
                                    Author - Adrian Miller

This book gives a comprehensive history of what has come to be known as soul food in America. The author discusses the complexities of how soul food has become incorporated into the American culture and gives a very detailed history of food associated with the soul food story.

AFRICAN AMERICAN HOSPITALITY INDUSTRY RECOMMENDED READINGS

THE AMERICAN COLORED WAITER, 1903 **Author - John B. Goins**

A manual to help others in the hospitality business learn how to set tables, how to carve meat, and specifically *"How to take it"*

THE WAITERS, 1953   **Author - William Fisher**

A novel about the trials and tribulations of an African American waiter in Manhattan, New York.

CUISINE NOIR MAGAZINE – The first food and wine lifestyle magazine for African Americans. On-line publication highlighting culinary traditions. www.cuisinenoirmag.com

RECOMMENDED HOSPITALITY MOVIES

"The Butler" - Produced by Lee Daniels

This movie honors the African American hospitality industry through the true story of Cecil Gaines, who was hired as a butler in the White House for over 34 years. He retired as head butler in 1986.

"The Help" – Story set in the 1960s which details the plight of domestic workers in the south during the Civil Rights movement.

"Guess Who's Coming to Dinner" – Comedy which challenges the attitudes of liberal white family whose daughter is engaged to an African American professional.

"Coming to America" – Comedy – African Prince (Eddie Murphy) comes to America to escape an arranged marriage and discovers the everyday life of African Americans in Harlem.
"Soul Food" – Comedy – The story of an African American family and the importance of their unity despite trials and misfortunes.

"Madea's Family Reunion" – Comedy – Movie written and produced by Tyler Perry which highlights the many issues that Madea's family encounters but manages to resolve them by supporting each other.
"Last Holiday" – Actress Queen Latifah discovers that she has a terminal illness and reflects on how she has lived her overly cautious life.

"Ms. Jane Pittman" – Actress Cicely Tyson portrays a 110-year-old ex-slave who tells her remarkable story of survival as she toiled on a plantation but arduously moved toward freedom, serving as an example of strength and resilience for generations to come.

"The Color Purple" - This movie is an epic tale of African American women who suffered abuse and toil in the South but managed to survive and maintain their family unity. Movie was based on book by author Alice Walker.

"Imitation of Life" – Actress Juanita Moore portrays a maid working in the of home of a struggling actress (Lana Turner) and their powerful relationship as mothers. This movie weaves together the complexities of racial tensions in America, human connections and the role and importance of service workers, so often overlooked.

EXHIBIT 8

SOUL FOODIES TO WATCH[15]

CHARLA L. DRAPER - FOOD CONSULTANT, OWNER of "It's Food Biz!" Provides marketing services promoting food and food related products in Chicago, Illinois.

CHEFS ON THE MOVE

Chef Byron Terry
"He is essentially an eco-friendly super-hero" quoted world renown chef Alice Waters. Bryant Terry is an African American vegan eco-chef, food justice activist, and author.

Chef Jeff Henderson
From humble beginnings in Los Angeles Chef Henderson became executive chef at the Bellagio Hotel and went on to host on the Food Network cable TV show.

Chef Haile Thomas
Ms. Thomas created a YouTube Channel – Kids Can Cook – after her father was diagnosed with Type 2 Diabetes. She has become a spokesperson for healthier eating. She has now become a public speaker on the subject and offers education on urban farming.

Celebrity Chef G. Garvin
Chef Garvin gives a simple, one size fits all approach to cooking that he has shared on his popular TV show and in his published cookbooks.

Celebrity Chef Joe Randall
Chef Joe Randall is a fifty-year veteran of the food service and hospitality industry and is recognized for his skills and ability in educating others in the field of culinary arts.

Chef Tiffany Derry

---

[15] http://anacostia.si.edu/exhibits/online_exhibitions/food/waiters_caterers_and_hoteliers.htm

Chef Tiffany Derry is a Dallas based Chef, well known for her appearance on TV's Top Chef cable food network competition. She is the national spokesperson for Arts Institute Culinary Arts Program.

Govind Armstrong

Chef Govind Armstrong created the 80 oz. Burger using his creative California cuisine style. He was raised on the Caribbean coast of Costa Rico. Chef Armstrong has opened several restaurants and is known for his wide range of southern cuisine.

Celebrity Chef Carla Hall

Chef Hall is a TV personality who was a finalist in show Top Chef. A native of Tennessee, Chef Hall now owns and operates her restaurant Southern Kitchen in New York.

Chef Carolyn Shelton

New Orleans Chef Shelton is author of several cookbooks and recent etiquette book Zydeco Blues and Gumbo. She lives in New Orleans and uses her knowledge to educate her community.

Celebrity Chef Marvin Woods

Chef Woods is an Emmy Award nominated television host and author of several Low Country cookbooks. He uses a healthy approach to cooking foods rooted in northern Africa, South America and the Caribbean.

Celebrity Chef Queen Vida M. Amuah

Queen Vida is an international Master Vegan Chef. With roots in West Africa, she has created heathy recipes for over 38 years. She is the author of vegan cookbook.

Carla Hall & Chef Willhoite

Chef Willhoite & Chef Michael Twitty

Chefs Willhoite, G. Garvin & Marvin Woods

**Chef Jeff Henderson
& Chef Willhoite**

**Chef Joe Randall &
Chef Willhoite**

EXHIBIT 9

AFRICAN AMERICAN OWNED RESTAURANTS

Everyone must do their part to help fellow entrepreneurs to survive.
Survival requires both individual and collective support

Just A Few "Must Visit" Restaurants

- **Sweet Home Café in The National African American History Museum, Washington D.C.** – The newest Smithsonian African American Museum 'made from scratch' food experience, opened in 2016. This experience is led by Chef Jerome Grant.
- **Lil Dizzy's Café – New Orleans, LA** – A Creole-Soul restaurant owned by Wayne Baquet and opened in 2005. He learned the business from his father Eddie Baquet who opened his legendary restaurant "Eddie's" that was known for its famous chicken.
- **The Praline Connection – New Orleans, LA** – A "down-home" Cajun Creole-Soul, home delivery food establishment known for its famous praline candy and authentic soul food.
- **Paschal's Restaurant – Atlanta, GA** – Opened in 1947 by the Paschal brothers, first operating out of their home in Atlanta. The restaurant became the local meeting place

in the 1960s for Civil Rights leader's strategy sessions, and the Paschal Brothers were known to post bond for jailed civil rights demonstrators. Paschal's now famous family fried chicken recipe is still the secret of their signature dish that keeps customers coming back for more.

- **Amy Ruth's – New York City** – Known for its famous Chicken and Waffles, this restaurant was inspired by a grandmother Amy Ruth Moore Bass. She was a mother of 10 children, a farmer, a gardener, and was reputed to be the best chicken cook in the world. One of the 10 children, Inez birthed a son who was destined to carry on his grandmother's love of good food and sharing the same joy that delighted her children. That grandson was Carl S. Redding who established Amy Ruth's restaurant in Harlem in 1999.

- **Red Rooster – Harlem, New York** – The Red Rooster is a restaurant created by Chef Marcus Samuelsson to honor the heart of the African American experience in New York – Harlem. It was named after a speakeasy that celebrated Black musicians during the Harlem Renaissance.

- **Sylvia's – New York** – Sylvia Woods, touted as the "Queen of Soul Food", created and founded Sylvia's Restaurant in Harlem, New York in 1962. In 2016 the street in front of the original restaurant, at 126th Street and Lenox Avenue was renamed in honor of this restaurateur – *Sylvia Woods Way*. Ms. Woods died in 2016.

- **Chicken George Restaurants** – Baltimore, Washington, D.C., Philadelphia – This chain of restaurants was very popular in the 1980's. Named after the character, "Chicken George" in the very popular TV miniseries, "Roots". Theodore Holmes founded 13 units in 1979. These restaurants are now closed. The most popular item on the menu was "The Gospel bird", a marinated spicy fried chicken. It was said that preachers always seemed to show up when there was fried chicken (the Gospel Bird) on the menu, during Sunday's Eat ins.

- **The Beautiful Restaurant – Atlanta, GA** - A Southern cuisine favorite spot in Atlanta, The Beautiful has served down home favorites for almost 40 years.

- **Big Daddy's Café & Restaurant – Atlanta, GA** – Home of the original Big Daddy's Dish Sausage, this cafeteria style restaurant is still a popular spot in Atlanta.

- **Rosco's Chicken & Waffles – Los Angeles, CA** – A local soul food chain serving signature chicken & waffles along with other southern favorites.

- **Busy Bee Cafeteria – Atlanta, GA** – This restaurant has been a staple of the community, serving local residents and students in the Atlanta University Center since 1947. Known for its popular fried chicken, this café is always packed.

- **Soul Delicious Restaurant – Morrow, GA** – A family owned, all you can eat buffet restaurant with a soulful environment including gospel music on Sundays.

- **Soul Vegetarian Restaurant** – Atlanta, GA – A southern style, meat free restaurant that has successfully operated in the West End Atlanta community for decades. This is the largest of a chain of restaurants run by members of the Israelite community of Jerusalem.

- **Weezy's Movin' On Up Café Jazz & BBQ** – Restaurant owned by the son of Isabel Sanford, actress who played character "Weezy" on popular TV sitcom The Jeffersons.

This restaurant, once a popular celebrity restaurant located outside of Atlanta, Ga in city of Johns Creek, is now closed.

So many African American restaurants struggle to stay in business for many reasons.

Most of these businesses start as small, mom & pop enterprises in a very aggressive business market. There are often restaurants on every other corner with whom these small business enterprises must continuously compete. Many of the competitors have corporate funds backing them, giving them the freedom to up their marketing games.

Over 10 years ago, African Americans were spending over 43 million dollars annually in Chinese Restaurants. Since that time those dollars have increased exponentially. Keeping our own businesses alive in our communities requires true support from our own people. Even some of the most popular restaurants often struggle to stay alive. By the time this book is published, some of this sampling of restaurants across the country mentioned in this book may no longer be in existence. We must continue to do our part to support our own.

There are approximately 832,000 African-American-owned businesses in the United States. Of those, at least two percent post annual revenue of $500,000 or more. According to the ING Gazelle Index, only five cents of every dollar spent by an African American-owned company was spent with other African-American vendors in 2002

| Singer Gladys Knight, former owner of Gladys Knight's & Ron Winans Chicken & Waffles Restaurant in Atlanta | Nick Ashford and Valerie Simpson, Owners of Sugar Bar Restaurant in New York City with Chef Willhoite | Known as "Florence" in the sitcom, "The Jeffersons", Marla Gibbs of Memory Lane Jazz Supper Club with Chef Willhoite |

EXHIBIT 10

AFRICAN AMERICAN CELEBRITY RESTAURANTS

Following the turn of the 20th century, the sale of church dinners, then the birth of small community delicatessens led to bigger and better places in which African Americans could dine. Soon there were restaurants, then hotels that continued the African American Soul Food stories. Built on the shoulders of African American small business owners, the growing popularity of entertainment and sports celebrities opened the door for the success of celebrity businesses, and the food service and hospitality industry birthed many.

Benzino's Crab Trap - located in Marietta, Georgia, this seafood restaurant is owned by former *Love & Hip-Hop* star, Benzino. The menu consists of corn and all his favorite crab dishes.

Ashford & Simpson's Sugar Bar - was opened in 1996 by Nicholas Ashford of the songwriting and performing duo, Ashford & Simpson. He and his wife Valerie Simpson opened their restaurant in Manhattan, New York, featuring good food, decadent desserts, and local music entertainment from R&B/Soul, Jazz, Caribbean, and traditional African rhythms.

Jay Z's 40/40 Club - opened in 2003 in New York by hip hop mogul Jay Z. Although it is sports-oriented, it reflects all the luxury of a fine New York restaurant. The menu includes favorites like Buffalo wings, sandwiches and salads, and mouth-watering house-made Bannoffe pie and warm Pineapple Upside down cake.

Michael Jordan's Steak House - located in Chicago, the restaurant features steak, crab cakes, grilled salmon, garlic bread and layered chocolate cake. It is considered one of the best steakhouses around and has locations in New York and Connecticut.

B.B. King Blues Club & Grill - located in New York in the heart of Times Square. This restaurant and blues club is a premier live music venue. Opened in the year 2000, B.B. King performed there many times until his death and hosted many other famous musicians there.

Gladys Knight Chicken & Waffles – Operated successfully in Atlanta, GA and in Maryland for many years, this restaurant was a popular family restaurant with several locations. The restaurant closed in 2016.

http://blog.blackbusiness.org/2015/08/top-black-owned-celebrity-restaurants.html

EXHIBIT 11

ANY EXCUSE TO CELEBRATE SOUL FOOD

National Martin Luther King Soul Food Competition
Muskogee, Oklahoma - *Soul Food Cook-Off held annually in Tulsa, Oklahoma in celebration of southern cooking.*

Soul Food Museum Day – November 11th

Declared by the city of Atlanta, Georgia at the opening of the Soul Food Museum on Auburn Avenue, which opened in 2008. Museum presently operates as a mobile unit in Atlanta. Established by Chef Dr. Kenneth Willhoite, Founder of the Soul Food Museum

Kwanzaa

Created in 1966 by Maulana Karenga, African American professor of Africana Studies , this holiday celebration emphasizes the seven Principles of an East African word "Kwanzaa" meaning "the first":

1. UMOJA (Unity)
2. KUJICHAGULIA (Self-determination)
3. UJIMA (Collective Work/Responsibility)
4. UJAMAA (Cooperative Economics)
5. NIA (Purpose)
6. KUUMBA (Creativity)
7. IMANI (Faith)

Kwanzaa - a secular festival observed by many African Americans from December 26 to January 1 as a celebration of their cultural heritage and traditional values.

Annual Collard Green Festival – Lithonia, GA – Festival to celebrate the history, traditions and foods of African Americans.

Annual Watermelon Party – Atlanta, GA – A 20+ year annual celebration of a favorite food of the African American community with its roots from West Africa. This annual celebration was created by Kwesi Jumoke Ifetayo.

National Soul Food Month – June

Sponsored by Culinary Historians of Chicago. Created to remind us to keep the soul food traditions alive, celebrating families who have passed down culinary soul food traditions from generation to generation.

Juneteenth - A combination of the word June and 19th – the day that the Emancipation of Slaves was celebrated in Texas in 1865. Although President Lincoln declared the emancipation, effective January 1, 1863, news traveled to the deep south very slowly. This news of freedom affected almost 250,000 slaves in rural Texas when Union General Gordon Granger stood on the Ashton Villa balcony in Galveston, Texas and announced the order of emancipation to all enslaved African Americans for the first time.

SOUL FOOD aka SOUTHERN CUISINE

"When we eat it, they call it Soul Food;
when White people eat it, they call it Southern Cooking"
Quote from Black Restaurateur – Quoted in Los Angeles Times, Oct. 11, 1984

Food that we now call Soul Food still includes what was considered the food of slaves and poor people – leftovers, scraps and other throwaways from the slave master's table. However, the inclusion of unique spices and other flavors from nature turned once undesirable food into "southern cuisine" – same food, different flavor. The very best of these prepared foods then became showcased at big plantation family gatherings and community celebrations. The same hands that prepared meals for slave families, prepared food for their owners, every day. Practice makes perfect and slave cooks gained plenty of experience, perfecting their crafts along the way. So, what became good for the goose became good for the gander, and vice versa. What the slaves were cooking in the "Big House" was the same food, at some point, that was being eaten in the slave quarters. Fried chicken, fried fish, biscuits, gravy, cornbread, jams, collard greens and more, became the regular cuisine for the slave and the master. However, to keep the necessary slave to master pecking order, the master's food had to be thought of as different and certainly better.

It was only after the emancipation of slaves, beginning in the early 1900s that African Americans had the freedom to proudly take ownership of their own culinary talents. They were now able to gather freely with family and friends, and start their own farms where they grew vegetables and tended animals used to feed their own families as well.

The Great Migration of African American families to the north and west brought new opportunities for some, and many hardships for others. Their food tastes stayed the same, but so many no longer had the luxury of fields of plants and vegetables and rivers within close proximity to catch fish for a good southern meal. The new world order in the big cities to which they migrated was more often a concrete jungle where fresh food was truly a luxury. A good down-home soul food feast was often costlier and was, therefore, saved for trips back down south.

Very often, a lack of something gives rise to new opportunities to fill the void for what might be lacking. So, during the 1920s, 1930s, 1940s and 1950s, African Americans who migrated north and west began opening small mom & pop restaurants and ethic neighborhood stores – satisfying the craving for "down home" southern cuisine aka soul food.

THE GREEN BOOK

As African American migrated from southern oppression to cities that were considered less oppressive, there was great difficulty in finding places to eat and lodge along this long journey. ***From lack comes creativity…*** Wendell P. Alston used this challenge as an opportunity to create **The Negro Motorist GREEN BOOK**. This book compiled lists of African American hotels, barbershops, beauty shops, boarding houses and restaurants where African American would be served without fear of retribution.

Over decades, as African Americans gained more freedoms, this necessary guidebook became less and less a travel necessity. Once considered inhuman and personal property, an entire race of people was now able to create a culture all their own – complete with their own music, their own businesses, their unique manner of cooking and more. To some degree, they now had recreated a New African – an African American.

———————————————————————

During the Montgomery, Alabama Boycott, an underground movement was started by **Georgia Gilmore** to raise money to support drivers for those refusing to ride buses until they received equal treatment under the law. Money raised from selling pies and other foods in beauty shops provided gas money for drivers and helped to buy station wagons to pick up passengers throughout Montgomery. Georgia Gilmore was among the unsung Civil Rights heroines who became a part of a story called "Hidden Kitchens" by NPR producers called "The Kitchen Sisters".

Like these "Hidden Kitchens", the Civil Rights Movement was built on strategy meetings in restaurants, ordinary family kitchens, and Black hotels across the country, including The Lorraine Motel where Martin Luther King lost his life at the hands of an assassin in 1968. It has been said that his last meal was a soul food meal complete with all his favorites including southern fried chicken with Louisiana hot sauce, black-eyed peas, collard greens and cornbread.

EXHIBIT 13

POPULAR AFRICAN AMERICAN GATHERING SPOTS EATERIES, HOTELS, CLUBS

African American eateries, hotels, and clubs in big cities offered selective menus with foods typical of their specific regions with an urban blend of the 'down home' soul food flavor. Music was a big draw for many patrons, particularly at spots like the **SAVOY BALLROOM** in New York City. Other popular clubs and eateries spotted across the country include the following:

ROYAL PEACOCK in Atlanta opened circa 1920 was originally a nightclub with two storefronts. The night club still exists with one storefront serving as a restaurant.

LA CAROUSEL JAZZ CLUB – Atlanta, GA Opened in 1960 as extension of the popular Atlanta Paschal's restaurant. It was considered Atlanta's jazz mecca for more than a decade. This club featured famous acts like Aretha Franklin, Lou Rawls, Dizzy Gillespie and more.

ALHAMBRA BALLROOM – A popular musical spot that opened in Harlem in 1926 and hosted musical legends such as Jelly Roll Morton and Bessie Smith. This event spot was restored in 2007.

THE APOLLO THEATER – HARLEM, NEW YORK – A musical venue opened in 1934 and helped to launch the musical careers of so many African American singers, dancers and musicians. The theatre became famous for its Amateur Night competitions, and still exists as one of the historic spots in the city.

SMALL'S PARADISE – NEW YORK – One of Harlem's most popular night clubs during the Harlem Renaissance. This was an African American owned club known for its on-stage entertainment featuring vocalizing and dancing waiters as well. The club was initially owned by Ed Smalls, but was later owned by basketball celebrity Wilt Chamberlain.

JACKSON WARD – RICHMOND, VA – 2ND AVENUE ("THE DEUCE") – Known as the Harlem of the South for its Black entertainment and business venues. This section of

Richmond attracted performers such as Duke Ellington, Ella Fitzgerald, Cab Calloway, Lena Horne and many others who traveled what became known as the ***"Chitlin' Circuit"*** – cities across the south known for its great entertainment.

THE BIG APPLE INN RESTAURANT in Jackson, Mississippi had the NAACP as an upstairs neighbor. The restaurant's owner, Mexico native Juan "Big John" Mora, was married to an African American woman. People who stopped in to buy hot sandwiches and tamales made from scratch often found Civil Rights leader Medgar Evers downstairs in the restaurant, mapping out protest strategies.

DOOKY CHASE RESTAURANT in New Orleans started hitting its stride in the late 1940s after jazz musician Edgar "Dooky" Chase married Leah Chase, a native of Madison, Louisiana. In the 1940s and '50s, the restaurant served musicians including Count Basie, Sarah Vaughn, Lena Horne, and Duke Ellington. In recent times, this restaurant even served the 44th President of the United States, Barak Obama.

Wife of New Orleans
Restauranteur Dooky Chase

Boxing Champion and Author of
"George Forman's Book of Grilling"

EXHIBIT 14

BLACK HOSPITALITY ENTREPRENEURS OF EIGHTEENTH & NINETEENTH CENTURIES

Our ancestors influenced many generations to become cooks, janitors, chefs, managers etc. who translated those skills into thriving businesses after the turn of the 20th century across America. Many African American entrepreneurs became very wealthy and created a new class of Black elite in many cities.

In the hospitality industry in the early and mid-1800s, free Black men and women used their experience in food preparation and service and their business knowledge to open successful catering businesses, restaurants and hotels. Even before the Civil War, the catering industry included many northern Blacks who had successful enterprises in cities such as Boston, Philadelphia and New York. Most Black hospitality businesses were supported by wealthy whites who valued the quality of service they received at these Black establishments. **Catering enterprises** often led to restaurant ownership and in some cases to the hotel business. George Downing, whose father owned an Oyster House in New York, opened his own Oyster House in the resort town of Newport, Rhode Island in 1846 and later built the luxurious Sea Girt Hotel on elegant Bellevue Avenue. Hospitality businesses ranged from single proprietors working from their homes to large establishments with sizeable staffs. In 1869, a group of twelve Black caterers formed the **Corporation of Caterers** as a way of supporting each other and insuring high standards among their membership. By 1870, the Corporation had 500 members including business owners and employees in the catering business. One of the best-known caterers in Philadelphia was Robert Bogel, a former waiter who became wealthy from his catering services.[16]

In the late 1800s, African Americans successful in the **catering business** joined forces and formed the United Public Waiters' Mutual Beneficial Association. In 1871, a Black family in Washington, D.C. opened The Wormley Hotel, named for their family. Their popular dining hall became one of the most fashionable restaurants in that area. Joseph Lee ran one of the most successful catering businesses in Boston, MA in 1890.

The Universal Negro Improvement Association and African Communities League (U.N.I.A – ACL) is a Black Nationalist fraternal organization founded in Jamaica 1914 by Marcus Garvey. Its membership increased to over 11 million with 1100 chapters in over 40 countries. This organization's mission was to uplift people of African ancestry through their charitable, educational, humanitarian and social interactions. The auxiliary components of this organization included Black Cross Nurses, Negro Factories Corporation, Black Eagle Flying Corp, Black Star Steamship Line, and more. Marcus Garvey led the largest Black organization in history.

The Honorable Marcus Mosiah Garvey and the members of the U.N.I.A -ACL unveiled what was to become the symbol of pride and honor for African Americans –

---

[16] https://blogs.scientificamerican.com/food-matters/eating-jim-crow/

The Red, Black and Green Flag whose colors stand for the blood that unites all people of African ancestry (red), Black people whose existence is confirmed by the flag, and abundant and natural wealth of Africa (green).

Another successful hospitality business enterprise that grew out of the Marcus Garvey organization was the Phyllis Wheatley Hotel in Harlem, New York.

Free Blacks were very enterprising using the skills and talents that they already knew, especially in northern cities. They worked as waiters, peddlers, innkeepers, cooks, vendors and more. Small diners and take-out shops opened across American in many small towns and in large cities like New York and Detroit.

THE TRUTH BEHIND
"Forty Acres and a Mule"

It is important to understand the significance of former slaves being able to first acquire land after the Emancipation Proclamation and then first build their homes and then their businesses. As the Civil War was coming to its end, Union General William T. Sherman and a group of Black ministers met in Savannah to discuss ways to help newly freed slaves. The plan was to set aside tillable land along the Southeast Coast of the Colonies for the freed slave families – not more than forty acres. This later became known as "Forty Acres and a Mule". However, after the assassination of President Lincoln, President Andrew Johnson reversed General Sherman's order and returned all of the land allotted to its former Confederate owners. The words "40 Acres and a Mule", live on, however, in the creative film works of Shelton Jackson "Spike" Lee – director, actor, producer, and writer.

EXHIBIT 15

AFFECTS OF JIM CROW ON SOUL FOOD & HOSPITALITY

The term "Jim Crow" was said to be inspired by an elderly Black handyman who had a shuffling gait and tendency to sing as he worked. Thomas Dartmouth Rice popularized the character in his enormously successful minstrel show. However, the term Jim Crow evolved to mean more than the character. By the late 1830s, it referred to the law that separated Blacks from Whites in public areas during the late nineteenth century. That included bus stations, restaurants, schools, stores, water fountains, and more.[17]

This law that enforced separation was both a blessing and a curse, depending on the perspective of the person interpreting this law. For self-sufficient African Americans, it meant establishing their own businesses, restaurants, schools, stores, banks and more. However, the struggle to keep their businesses and schools was an uphill climb because of the lack of financial support. Despite the struggle, there were many successful ventures that sprung up across America in the small towns that were also built by African Americans with the help of the U.S. Bureau of Refugees, Freedmen and Abandoned Lands. This was also known also as **The Freedmen's Bureau** created by the U.S. Congress in 1865 to aid freed slaves and refugees at the end of the Civil War. In 1910, there was a peak in land ownership for Blacks. Collectively Blacks owned 15 million acres of land of which 218,000 Black farmers were full or part owners. A steady decline of land ownership began after 1910. It was over 50 more years before farmers could get a strong foothold to build their agricultural businesses. In 1967, **the Federation of Southern Cooperatives** was founded to aid in the economic development for Black farmers and the rural poor. It was one continuous mountain climb after another for African Americans trying to rebuild millions of their lives that for centuries, had been in bondage. Almost 400 years later, despite progress, the struggle continues.

---

[17] Black Towns Established by Freed Slaves After the Civil War; Are Dying Out. The Washington Post Newspaper, Deneen L. Brown, March 27, 2015

EXHIBIT 16

ALL BLACK TOWNS BUILT IN AMERICA

Following the Emancipation Proclamation issued by President Lincoln in 1862, buying land was so important for these newly freed people. *"They would build buildings, whether it was a home or a fellowship hall."* Because many of these former slaves were working to earn a living during the day, they would raise community buildings at night. *"There is a story of one church where the women would hold lanterns, so the men could work in the dark."*[18] These foundations of growth and development paved the way for education and businesses that would improve the lives of freed African Americans. These towns were the pillars of hope for an entire culture of people.

Some of the original Black towns were **Blackdom, New Mexico, Hobson City, Alabama, Allensworth, California,** and **Rentiesville, Oklahoma.** Because residents did not record their existence and their experiences, and whites were not interested in preserving and collecting material on these Black towns, much information about some of these towns that were founded by these former slaves has been lost.

Oklahoma's all-Black towns included **Clearview, Boley** (established in 1905 on Creek Indian territory and later known nation-wide for its annual BBQ festivals and rodeos) and **Langston,** which were founded around 1890, according to the Black Towns Project.

The list of all Black towns in American established after emancipation is impressive. Many were unincorporated and never recorded for historical record. However, those towns crisscross America from the Atlantic to the Pacific Oceans and from the Canadian Borders to South America. Some worth additional note includes: **New Philadelphia, Illinois** founded in 1836 many years before the end of the Civil War out in the Midwestern frontier. **Buxon, Iowa** was a multi-racial town, but African Americans far outnumbered the other ethnic groups. One of the most amazing successes for Black towns was established in the last place in America one would expect – Mississippi. **Davis Bend, MS** was established as a self-governing town of 350 former slaves on land that was previously a plantation. The town did not survive, but the son of original founder Benjamin Montgomery, Isaiah Montgomery, went on to found Mound Bayou,

---

[18] What was Americas first Black Town by Henry Louis Gates – Originally posted on THE ROOT, 100 Amazing Facts About Negroes

Mississippi in 1887. Today, Mound Bayou has one of the largest African American communities in the United States.

These all Black towns built hotels, eating establishments, post offices, farms, grocery stores, schools and more. They built a foundation upon which they could sustain their families with an agricultural and service base that would ultimately change the lives of hundreds of thousands of people -- giving them new lives, new skills, new dreams.

It was during this time that African Americans began to make a significant mark on the agriculture business in American – creating farmland on which they grew their own vegetables and fruits to take care of their own families and to sell in the ever-expanding marketplace. However, the struggle to keep their farmland was continuous. A few government programs existed between 1886 – 1920 to boost agricultural opportunities for Black farmers and sharecroppers. Because Black farmers were unable to get bank loans to finance equipment and supplies needed to keep their farmland, not a significant number of Black farmers succeeded. However, a few were able to make some inroads.

As the number of Black towns grew across America, so did opportunities in not only agriculture, but also more in the hospitality and food industry.

––––––––––––––––––––––––––––––––––––––

. "The **Black Wall Street** of America" was the **Greenwood District of Tulsa, Oklahoma** in the early twentieth century. The race riot of 1921 in Tulsa destroyed people, property, hopes and dreams. The town was burned to the ground by whites and the Black citizens were run out of town. The Greenwood District pioneers, however, rebuilt the community from ashes. By 1942, there were 242 businesses in the Greenwood District.

BLACK WALL STREET
Tulsa, Oklahoma

––––––––––––––––––––––––––––––––––––––

MOUND BAYOU, MISSISSIPPI was founded in 1887 by freedmen led by former slave Isaiah Montgomery. The town, according to blackpast.org, was designed for the residents to have very little contact with whites. It had a post office, churches, banks, schools and stores and was often cited by Booker T. Washington as a model of self-sufficiency. **Mound Bayou**, Mississippi still exists today. **Freedmen's Town near Houston, TX** was dubbed "Little Harlem". Like many others, this town also did not survive but went on to be designated as an historic district.

FREEDMAN'S VILLAGE, VIRGINIA - Built in 1863, this town was the home of several notable African Americans, including Sojourner Truth who settled there in 1864. She worked there as a teacher and helped residents find jobs. The town existed until 1900 when the land was taken by the government as the site for Arlington National Cemetery, the Navy Annex and the Pentagon.

FREEDMAN'S VILLAGE, VIRGINIA

SUGARLAND, MARYLAND – Established October 1871 when three freed slaves bought land from a former slave owner

The Sugarland Well. Children in the background are (l-r): Mary Smith, Marjorie Lee, Sarah Lee, Tilghman Lee, Jr., Idella Lee. The adult in the foreground is Samuel Jackson.
Photo courtesy of the St. Paul Community Church Archives.

SUGARLAND, MARYLAND

CHAPEL HILL, MARYLAND - Many of the Black communities were tight-knit, rural, and centered around school and church, said Susan Pearl, a historian at the Prince George's County Historical Society in Maryland. *"Little communities formed. The first thing they would build was a church or a Freedman's Bureau school. That happened in Chapel Hill"*, a community in Prince George's County that freed Blacks founded in 1868. A few other original families remain, she said, but *"all the younger people are moving out. As they widen the roads, property is being lost. People who are moving in don't have the same passion for Chapel Hill that the originals do…. The history is being lost."*

CHAPEL HILL, MARYLAND

Sometime between March and November of 1738, Spanish settlers in Florida formed a town called **GRACIA REAL DE SANTA TERESA MOSE**. The town was just north of St. Augustine, Florida and was established by 38 men and their families who were fugitive slaves who fled to Florida for sanctuary. They had been slaves in Georgia and the Carolina. The town later became known as **Fort Mose**.[19]

NICODEMUS, KANSAS – Advertised as The Largest Colored Colony in America. The town of Nicodemus invited freed slaves to Kansas with this ad: *"All Colored People that want to go to Kansas, on September 5th, 1877, can do so for $5.00."*

---

[19] The History of Lost Black Towns, http://www.theroot.com/historys-lost-black-towns-1790868004

NICODEMUS, KANSAS

What is now Bedford-Stuyvesant in Brooklyn, New York, **WEEKSVILLE** was the second-largest community for free Blacks prior to the Civil War. James Weeks, a freed slave, bought a significant amount of land from Henry C. Thompson, another freed slave. Weeks sold property to new residents, who eventually named the community after him. It thrived over the years, becoming home to both southern Blacks fleeing slavery and northern Blacks escaping the racial violence and riots in New York and other cities.[20]

ALLENSWORTH, CA - In 1908, Lt. Col. Allen Allensworth and four others set up the California Colony and Home Promoting Association with the mind-set of establishing the state's first all-Black township. Located on the Santa Fe rail line, by 1914, the town housed the first Black school district, judicial system and a hotel in the face of setbacks like water-supply issues and closing of the railroad stop in their town. The township is now preserved as Colonel Allensworth State Historic Park.[21]

---

20 The History of Lost Black Towns, http://www.theroot.com/historys-lost-black-towns-1790868004
21 The Soul Makeover. Today's Dietician Magazine. November 2013

ROSEWOOD, FLORIDA - Established in 1870, town was considered the site of the worse race riot in U.S. history. In 1923, a white woman claimed she had been sexually assaulted by a Black man. The town was destroyed by a band of white men; the number of Black residents killed is still unknown.

ROSEWOOD, FLORIDA

SENECA VILLAGE, NEW YORK - This town of prominent African American property owners existed between 1825-1857. The town had 254 residents who built three churches, a school and several cemeteries. The town was razed, and this history erased when it was replaced by New York's Central Park.

SENECA VILLAGE, NEW YORK

EXHIBIT 17

HEALTH CHANGES & THE FUTURE OF SOUL FOOD COOKING

As Americans strive to create healthier bodies with exercise, improved sleeping habits and changes in eating habits, soul food, as we have known it over the years, has been blamed for poor health trends in African American families. This includes heart attacks, high blood pressure, diabetes, gout and more. Those with that concern point to the high fat and sugar content used in many soul food dishes.

Although this argument holds some merit, without question, those who truly love soul food are determined not to "throw out the baby with the bath water". Passionate soul food lovers like me chose to make changes that do not change the entire flavor of what has fed, nourished and uplifted African Americans spirits for over 400 years.

There are now salt and sugar substitutes that can be used without totally altering the flavor of many of our favorite dishes. Instead of pork in collards greens, many great cooks now use turkey, and families are nonetheless satisfied after their meals.

Here are a few of my personal favorite changes that are being shared across the U.S.:

- In Kentucky, a program was started among 40 parishes to encourage healthier eating with the Harriett B. Porter Culinary Institute for African American churches. It was named in honor of Harriett Porter, health advocate and educator by her surviving family to encourage church leadership to help parishioners to eat healthier. Each of the churches post nutrition tips in church bulletins and they receive a copy of the New American Heart Health Cookbook and a stipend to implement a nutrition program in each church.[22]

- Filmmaker Byron Hurt states in his interview with Ebony Magazine *"Byron Hurt Serves Up Healthy Soul Food"*, that there is nothing inheritably wrong with soul food, but how you prepare the soul food. In his movie "Soul Food Junkie" Hurt offers alternative ways of cooking soul food, for example, instead of frying chicken, peel the skin off and bake it. Instead of eating candied yams, bake that sweet potato. Instead of cooking collard greens for hours in a fatty ham hock, cook a shorter time and sauté the greens using olive oil, garlic and combinations of other spices.[23]

- The Academy of Nutrition and Dietetics recommends reinventing some traditional family recipes[24]. For example:

> Create juicy, crispy "oven-fried" chicken by soaking it in buttermilk then coating with a blend of panko breadcrumbs, paprika, garlic powder and cayenne pepper before baking with a spritz of canola oil.

> Slow cook greens in vegetable broth with a drizzle of canola or peanut oil. Sweeten the pot with honey and apple cider vinegar. For the adults, add red pepper flakes or hot sauce. If collard or turnip greens are too bitter for your child's palate, try a cabbage, which cooks up a bit sweeter. Serve with skinny, baked cornbread sticks for a fun and nutritious meal.

> Instead of fried okra, roast fresh whole okra until crunchy and dip into your favorite marinara sauce.

> You don't have to give up peach cobbler. Bake peaches with honey and top with oats, toasted almonds and a dollop of vanilla Greek yogurt.

The food and hospitality industry in America continues to change and grow exponentially. The African American contributions to this industry are growing right along with it as more products are added to food shelves across this country, many with healthier options. There are now only a handful of African American Food Manufacturers in the U.S.:

- Glory Foods, Inc. - Southern Style Cooking founded in 1989; has over 85 products

---

[22] Byron Hurt Serves Up Healthy 'Soul Food'. EBONY Magazine by Jamilah Lemieux, January 14, 2013
[23] EAT RIGHT – Academy of Nutrition and Dietetics. "Healthy Soul Food, Your Way" http://www.eatright.org/resource/health/lifestyle/culture-and-traditions/healthy-soul-food-your-way
[24] Stuff You Should Know On-line Blog. http://www.stuffyoushouldknow.com/

- Truly Corporation – Marinade Seasoning used as alternative to barbecue sauce
- Annabelle's Soul Food Seasoning – All in One Seasoning
- Good-2-Go Ready Meals
- Bridge Foods, Inc.
- Oprah Winfrey Food Line (In partnership with Kraft/Heinz Company) – launched 2017 called *O, That's Good!* Mashed Potatoes, Three Cheese Pasta, Parmesan Pasta
- Sylvia Woods Food Line- Canned Vegetables, Sauces, Spices, Dessert Mixes

In Volume II of The Soul Food Museum, I will chronicle the many products produced by African Americans that have sprung from the food manufacturing industry in America. This Soul Food Directory will give a continental 'Tour Guide' for shoppers searching specifically for soul food Products. ***Stay Tuned!***

EXHIBIT 18

LITTLE KNOWN FACTS RELATED TO SOUL FOOD AND HOSPITALITY INDUSTRY...

- In 1846, a Louisiana slave gardener was the first to successfully grow pecan trees.
- The hospitality industry in Georgia encompasses more than 18,500 restaurants employing more than 275,000 people in a range of positions. For the United States, the National Restaurant Association estimates that food sales in 2004 topped $400 billion in more than 878,000 locations.
- "Culinary" can mean everything from a short-order cook to what we consider the executive head chef who brings a very high salary in five-star hotels, country clubs and non-restaurant settings. There are just so many different areas and so many different tiers in the culinary arena that it's good for the job market."
- Alex Haley – world-renowned author and creator of the "Roots" TV saga, was a cook while serving in the U.S. Navy.
- Chaka Khan had her own gourmet chocolate candy named "Chakalat's".
- Ray Charles, a legend with such top hits as "You are my Sunshine", "America the Beautiful" and "Georgia on my Mind", loved cooking his own meals, especially fried chicken, even though he lost his sight as a child.
- Cola has often been an expected drink at the soul food table, and rightly so, because the Kola Nut is the fruit of the Kola Tree – native to the rain forest of Mother Africa. This became the flavoring agent for all "colas".
- "The Cake Walk" was a dance event that originated during slavery in the 19th century. Slaves were invited to dress up and dance for the master. Slaves used this opportunity to mimic and mock the "airs" of this southern aristocracy. The winner of this dance would be given a cake for their performance.[25]

---

[25] The Terrible Transformation, GPB/PBS African American Resource Teacher Guide http://www.pbs.org/wgbh/aia/part1/1p263.html

- To grow chestnuts, you must plant the male female trees side by side, for them to bear the fruit of the nut. Interestingly enough, the same mating requirement applies to some species of pecan trees.
- Marla Gibbs – Actress, comedian, singer; known as the maid on the hit TV show "The Jefferson's" and her own TV show "227" owned her own restaurant in Los Angeles, California called Marla Gibbs' Memory Lane Jazz Supper Club. Her delicious spiced carrot cake is her most notable dessert.
- Dick Gregory – world-renowned comedian, humanitarian, author and health guru educated Americans about their health until his death I 2017. He's most commonly known for "The Bahamian Diet" and the promotion of the "George Washington Carver products" using the recipes of famed Dr. George Washington Carver of Tuskegee Institute. The Bahamian Diet supplement has a variety of vegan ingredients including rice and flaxseed powder, coffee bean, bitter melon and milk thistle extract, mango and lime fruit powder, pepper and even turmeric root. It has come to be known also as a weight loss product
- Rapper Nelly's "Pimp Juice" sold over a million units in less than four months, despite some public protest.
- Our use of soap, cooking oil, margarine and lotion made from refined and processed coconut oil is credited to the inventor of the biscuit cutter, Alexander Ashebourne.
- The first slave ship docked near Jamestown, Virginia in 1619 with cooks, servants, approximately 20+ indentured slaves. There are competing arguments as to whether the first Africans in America were indentured workers or slaves. It is agreed that there were slaves that came to American prior to 1619 with explorers from Europe. Whether their status was simply as a servant or as slave is still being debated.[26]
- The black cast iron skillet was the favorite cooking utensil for Black cooks in the 1800's, and remains a favorite for so many Black cooks today.
- Reverend Jesse Jackson, civil rights activist, improved employment opportunities in the industry by boycotting restaurants that would not hire Black managers. He keeps "HOPE" alive. Rev. Al Sharpton worked with Rev. Jackson at Operation Breadbasket in Chicago, Illinois and New York City.
- Mahalia Jackson, renowned gospel singer, not only loved gospel, but she also loved to cook. In fact, she along with Benjamin L. Hooks started and operated a franchise called Mahalia Jackson's Chicken Franchise in the 1960's.
- Bussey Florist is the first Black FTD Florist in Metro Atlanta offering worldwide services. James & Alice Bussey have owned and operated Bussey Florist since 1962, paving the road for many others in the hospitality industry.
- Civil Rights leader Andrew Young, whose roots began in his hometown of New Orleans, Louisiana, is known also for his great gumbo.

---

[26] The Splendid Table – Black Presidential Cooks in the White House: Their Stories. Podcast. https://www.splendidtable.org

- The National African American Culinary Arts & Hospitality Association held its inauguration on June 28, 2003 at the Georgia World Congress Center in Atlanta, Georgia. It was founded by Chef Dr. Kenneth Willhoite.

- Isaac Hayes a musician, actor, radio personality, philanthropist, composer and the voice of Chef on the Animated TV show "South Park". He was also known to be a great cook and passed the gift down to his son.

- The first African American cook in the White House was a slave named Hercules, who cooked for the first U.S. President George Washington. He later became the cook in George Washington's personal residence as well.[27]

- Prince Hall, one of Boston's most prominent citizens during the revolutionary period, was the founder of the African Lodge of the Honorable Society of Free and Accepted Masons of Boston, the world's first lodge of Black Freemasonry. Prince Hall was a caterer & huckster. He arrived in Boston from Africa. Born circa 1765, he went on to found what would become "Prince Hall Grand Lodge of Massachusetts.[28]

- International Chef Queen Vida Amuah of Ghana Africa was crowned on May 20th, 2016 at the Georgia State Capitol as the World Queen of Soul Food.

- James Brown, dubbed "King of Soul" and businessman, was known worldwide. He also owned the Golden Skillet Restaurant chain and created a line of cookies.

- Ms. Nobantu Ankoanda, Ed. D created the Annual Collard Green Cultural Festival in Atlanta, Georgia and the Collard Green Ice Cream. The festival began in California.

- In the 1920s, the Pullman Company was the largest employer of African American men on trains crossing America. The Pullman Porters brought a sense of class and prestige to the railroad, offering first class hospitality by serving passengers -- preparing their compartments, shining shoes at night, and giving other valued hospitality services. The railroad hired the cooks and waiters in the dining cars on the trains.[29]

- "G.O.A.T." (Greatest of All Time) Food & Beverage Company was created by two inspired individuals: legendary champion Muhammad Ali and brand inventor Peter Arnell." "*…dedicated to optimally serving young adults revolutionary new foods, snacks and beverages that provide functional benefits, great taste, lifestyle enhancement and nutritional needs.*"

- Eating white dirt (rock called Kaolin) found along the Atlantic coastline, is a southern states tradition, mostly found in female African American community.

- Born in 1844, Cathay Williams was a slave who served under General Sherman when the Civil War broke out. She was freed by the union soldiers. The army recruited her as a cook and laundress. After the war, she moved to Virginia and joined the 38th U.S. Infantry (Buffalo Soldiers) in 1866, pretending to be a man. Cathay Williams was honorably discharged on October 14, 1868, having made her place in history as the first

[27] GPB Resource Bank. www.gpb.org. The Revolution – People and Events: Prince Hall 1765- 1807

[28] America on the Move – Pullman Porters and Maids Helping Passengers. American History Museum

[29] African American Registry. Cathay Williams – Buffalo Soldier B http://www.aaregistry.org/historic_events/view/cathy-williams-buffalo-soldier-bornorn.

female Buffalo Soldier to serve. Growing tired of the army she feigned illness and it was then discovered that she was a female and discharged in 1868.[30]

- Bean pie is a sweet custard pie whose filling consists of mashed beans, usually navy bean, sugar, eggs, milk, butter, and spices. The pies are also associated with the Nation of Islam movement and Elijah Muhammad, who encouraged their consumption instead of richer foods generally associated with soul food.

- During the mid to late 1800s, African Americans dominated the catering business. In 1869, they formed the United Public Waiters' Mutual Beneficial Association to check the services of the waiters and of the food services they provide.

- The original Queen of Soul Food, Sylvia Woods, went from picking beans in the fields of a small rural town in South Carolina to owning Manhattan's oldest and world respected soul food restaurant – *Sylvia's*. The restaurant feeds millions around the globe every year.

- Debbie Allen, actress, dancer, and T.V. and movie director owned a restaurant in Los Angeles along with her husband, Norm Nixon – legendary L.A. Lakers basketball player. They love entertaining friends and family with their specialty dishes of apple smoked filet mignon with ginger snapped string beans.

- Marcus Garvey, who advocated that African Americans return to their homeland, Africa He began a self-help organization for oppressed Black people in America. He worked as a janitor before starting his national organization.

- Ervin "Magic" Johnson bought a Pepsi-Cola distribution plant in Forestville, Maryland with the help of Black Enterprise Publisher Earl G. Graves. By 1999 "Magic" had opened 8 Starbuck stores, T.G.I. Friday and Fat Burger Restaurants, a 24-hour sports club and the Magic Johnson Theatres.

- Reginald F. Lewis was the riches African American man in 1980, In 1987 he brought Beatrice International Foods for $985 million dollars.

- The unofficial snack of Hip Hop was created by James "Fly" Linsey in 1994 with Lil Romeo. The company that produced them was "Rap Snacks" potato chip company,

- Sidney Poitier worked in hospitality as a dishwasher before becoming an actor.

- The sweet potato which is indigenous to America, is often confused with the yam that originated in Africa. They are from two completely different plant families.

- Jamel Frazier, better known as actor "Buckwheat" was the nephew of Blues singer Bessie Smith, lived in San Fernando, CA and fathered four children. His famous character name was borrowed from a flour sack and was one of the most recognized faces from the 'Little Rascals' comedy series.

- LaWanda Page, TV personality better known as "Aunt Esther" on Sanford and Sons comedy show, was also call "Old Fish Eyes" by Red Foxx because she enjoyed fish and grits for breakfast.

- The popular alcoholic beverage Jack Daniel, was name after founder Jasper "Jack" Daniel. However, Mr. Daniel learned his trade from enslaved African American Nathan "Nearest"

---

30 Miles, Michael. "Black Cooperatives. The New Republic September 21, 1968

Green who was a master moonshine distiller. Mr. Green continued to work with the company after he was emancipated from slavery in 1865.

- Shaquille O'Neal, retired basketball player, recognized at once as "Shaq" has released a line of beverages (in four flavors) that are sold a 7-11 convenience stores.
- Even when celebrities fall from grace, they often continue to be linked to the product that they so successfully endorsed when most popular. Case in point, Bill Cosby will be forever attached to Jell-O Pudding Pops and Orenthal James (O.J.) will be remembered as representative for Hertz Rent-a-Car Service and Wheaties cereals.
- "Snoop Dog", famous Rapper, Snoop's Potluck Dinner Party with co-host Martha Stewart, TV chef and business woman.
- Atlanta is the home of what has been dubbed as "The World's Greatest Ghetto Burger" at Ann's Snack Bar, an old school counter serve spot made famous because of its burger.

MORE FOOD FACTS THAT YOU MAY NOT KNOW….

African American celebrities have influenced the food and hospitality industry in so many ways from the mid-20th century until the present day. Well-known faces are often the driving force in the success of businesses and that certainly holds true for African American businesses in the food and hospitality industry.

In addition to celebrities mentioned previously in this book, many persons of note have had major impact on my life. I could not complete this book without mentioning those who I feel have changed the fabric of our lives in so many different and important ways.

As a music lover, I have had a special interest in knowing the palate favorites of some of my most loved artists:

Quincy Jones is well known for his excellent barbecue ribs; Aretha Franklin, whose favorite pastime is cooking, helped Barry Gordy's mom cook for the Motown family. Her signature dish was Peach Cobbler. Another Motown artist, Smokey Robinson introduced a successful Seafood Gumbo for purchase in stores.

Now, 84 years of age and a still active vegetarian, Richard Penniman, better known as "Little Richard" worked in the hospitality industry as a dishwasher before he became a legendary entertainer. His songs Tutti Fruitti, Lucille, and Good Golly Miss Molly are instantly recognized and associated with Little Richard. Today he continues to perform and does commercials for Taco Bell.

Michael Jackson, who became a world renowned singer/performer, but known simply by his children as the best French Toast maker around. He was known to have a sweet tooth that started in his mother's kitchen as he loved sampling her sweet potato pies.

Because I now call Atlanta, Georgia my home, I could not omit the celebrity influences on food and hospitality in a town that loves and supports this industry like no other:

One of the most popular restaurants in Atlanta is owned and operated by local radio personality Frank Ski whose business carries his name. In 2016 popular rapper, Ludacris opened his Chicken and Beer restaurant at one of the largest airports in the world – Hartsfield-Jackson International Airport. Still benefiting from its long-term popularity at the Atlanta airport is the historic Paschal's restaurant. For Low Country cuisine at the airport, travelers can now dine at Chef G. Garvin's LowCountry restaurant. Also at Atlanta's Hartsfield-Jackson airport is 'Chicken & Beer' Restaurant owned by Rapper/Actor Ludacris. Rapper T.I. opened is upscale Soul Food restaurant just a few miles away in downtown Atlanta.

Cashing in on the draw for afterhours clubs and restaurants, crooner Keith Sweat opened his restaurant in 1996 shortly before Soul Food Queen, Sylvia Woods and Gladys Knight and her brother Ron opened their restaurants in the late 1900s. In 1999 famous boxer, Evander Holyfield opened his New South Grill. It stayed open a little over a year.

On corners throughout Atlanta, Muslim brothers can be seen selling their popular Bean Pies and other popular dishes in Muslim restaurants in the metropolitan Atlanta area.

Now an Atlanta resident, singer Bobbie Brown has been successfully marketing his tasty Bobby's BBQ Sauce along with his other seasoning creations sold under LLC Bobby Brown Foods.

Soul Food was a mainstay for Civil Rights 'soldiers'. It is well known that Dr. King loved a good soul food meal -- whether eating his wife Coretta's popular collard greens, having a real down-home soul food meal at Paschal's restaurant during their Civil Rights strategy sessions, or his very last meal in Memphis, Tennessee.

Not far from his Atlanta roots, Heisman Trophy winner Herschel Walker founded Renaissance Man Food Services, Inc. in 2009 in Savannah, Georgia. It is one of the largest minority-owned meat processing businesses in the nation, which includes a chicken processing plant and pre-cooked ribs for hotels, restaurants and the military.

Like fellow entertainer Pattie LaBelle with her Pattie Pies line of foods, television celebrity Steve Harvey is now successfully marketing his food line of Roasted Bacon in Wal-Mart stores throughout the United States.

The list of Black celebrity cook books is long, but just a few worth noting are: Patti LaBelle's Recipes for the Good Life; George Forman's Indoor Grilling Made Easy; Ziggy Marley's Family Cookbook; rapper Coolio's Cookin' with Coolie: 5 Star Meals at a 1 Star Price; Oprah's Favorite's – In the Kitchen with Rosie; Maya Angelou's Great Food All Day Long; Laila Ali's Food for Life; Pastor T.D. Jakes' Woman Thou Art Loosed Cookbook; and Al Roker's Big Bad Book of Barbecue.

There are many celebrities who simply love good food, and they enjoy preparing and sharing it with friends and family. Some noted down-home cooks were author of historical narrative "Roots", Alex Haley, talented singer Luther Vandross, and Civil Rights icon Dorothy Height, who was said to love sweet potatoes for breakfast, lunch and dinner.

Gone, but not forgotten are restaurateurs Josephine Baker, famous international persona, Lloyd Price, R& B singer who had a line of breakfast cereals, energy bars, and cookies, and the world's beloved singer and consummate entertainer Prince who was a soulful vegetarian.

The first Black president of The National Restaurant Association is Herman Cain, who also ran unsuccessfully for President of the United States in 2012, and who was Chairman and CEO of Godfather's Pizza where he served for a decade.

Established in 1941, New Orleans family owned restaurant, Dooky Chase's, became nationally known. It was named for the family patriarch, Dooky Chase who died in 2016. Like Paschal's in Atlanta, Dooky Chase was a hotspot for Civil Rights strategists and was frequented by politicians and freedom fighters over meals in the restaurant's upstairs meeting rooms.

Oprah Winfrey has gained her celebrity as an entertainment mogul but also has a passionate love of food. In 1989, her restaurant Eccentric opened to huge patronage and stayed open until 1995.

Other celebrities who ventured into the restaurant business include singer Stephanie Mills, golfer Tiger Woods, and R&B base guitar icon, Bootsy Collins, NBA basketball star Earvin "Magic" Johnson, former Ikette (Of Ike & Tina R& B Review) Robbie Montgomery (Owner of "Sweetie Pie's" in St. Louis, Missouri), and baseball hero Hank Aaron, who is owner of several fast food franchises.

Many stars have been honored with their personalized cakes and pastries at Kenya's Cakes of the Stars in Los Angeles, CA. Owner Kenya Jackson, daughter of Gladys Knight created her gourmet cakes for her mother, Dionne Warwick, Pattie LaBelle and Natalie Cole in 1994, however, this business is now closed.

Annual Soul Food Museum Awards Celebration – In 2002 the Soul Food Museum (Atlanta, GA) held its Inaugural celebration at the Georgia World Congress Center to honor America's top African Americans working in the field of culinary arts, hospitality and agriculture. This is the first event of this type and magnitude to honor those working in these fields.

In 2016 this annual event was dedicated in memory of The Godfather of Soul, James Brown and artist Prince for their contributions to the culinary and hospitality industry. This event was held at the Georgia State Capitol in Atlanta. 2017 will mark the 15th year of this celebration.

Sarah Breedlove, better known as Madam C. J. Walker, was an African American entrepreneur and philanthropist who was a self-made millionaire who tremendously impacted the hospitality industry.

The Soul Food Museum continues to celebrate our contributions of African Americans in these industries beginning in 1619, almost 400 years of ***"Building on the Legacy of Our Ancestors"***, which is the motto of the Soul Food Museum.

From coast to coast we recognize and honor the men and women serving tirelessly in the fields of culinary arts, hospitality, and agriculture including the following:

- COOKS
- CHEFS
- WAITERS
- WAITRESSES
- BUTLERS
- WAREWASHERS/DISHWASHERS
- MIXOLOGISTS/BARTENDERS
- CATERERS
- RESTAURANT & HOTEL OWNERS/OPERATORS
- FOOD & DRINK MANUFACTURERS

- SHOE SHINERS
- AIRLINE HOSTS & HOSTESSES
- COMMUNITY GROCERY STORE OWNERS/OPERATORS
- CHAUFFEURS
- FARMERS
- BUS & TRAIN OPERATORS
- CITY & STATE OFFICIALS

Since African American came to the American shores almost 400 years ago, they have contributed to the growth and creative development of the culinary arts, agriculture and hospitality industries. The Soul Food Museum will continue to honor those who have given and continue to give their talents, their passion and their toil in doing what they love.

Historically Black Colleges & Universities (HBCUs) have, over the past years, added programs to encourage African American students to consider career paths in the Food and Hospitality industries. The following HBCUs have established successful programs in this area:

- UNIVERSITY OF MARYLAND EASTERN SHORE
- NORTH CARROLINA CENTRAL UNIVERSITY
- MORGAN STATE UNIVERSITY
- VIRGINIA STATE UNIVERSITY
- TUSKEGEE UNIVERSITY
- DELAWARE STATE UNIVERSIY
- HOWARD UNIVERSITY
- GRAMBLING STATE UNIVERSITY
- HAMPTON UNIVERSITY
- BETHUNE COOKMAN UNIVERSITY
- CHEYNEY UNIVERSITY OF PENNSYLVANIA
- UNIVERSITY OF THE DISTRICT OF COLUMBIA
- TOUGALOO COLLEGE
- ST. PHILIP'S COLLEGE
- COAHOMA COMMUNITY COLLEGE

CONTINUING THE CELEBRATION OF
THE SOUL FOOD MUSEUM

Boxing Champion Muhammad Ali.
He started several restaurant businesses

Activist & Health Food
Advocate Dick Gregory

Singer & Cook Pattie LaBelle
Created Pattie Pies

Rainbow Push, Operation Breadbasket
Leader & Social Activist Jessie Jackson

Irving Magic Johnson – Former
Basketball Star and Entrepreneur –
Owned several food franchises

Henry "Hank" Aaron Hall of Fame
Baseball Star & owner of several
food franchises in Atlanta

Motown Music Moguls Smokey Robinson & Motown Founder Barry Gordy

Singer/Entrepreneur James Brown aka "Godfather of Soul" founded a fast food franchise called James Brown's Gold Platter

Civil Rights Activist & Baptist Minister Al Sharpton has been touted as "the voice of the voiceless and a champion for the down trodden" by former President Barack Obama

Herman Cain, First African American
President of the National Restaurant
Association & CEO of Godfather's Pizza

Al Roker, NBC News Anchor/Weatherman
with Chef Kenneth Willhoite

Friends of the Soul Food Museum: (L) Rev. Joseph Lowery and
(R) Rev. C.T. Vivian – Iconic Civil Rights Activists

Chef Scott Peacock, author of memoir about African American Souther Chef Edna Lewis, honored here by Chef Willhoite

Former TV Talk Show Host Tavis Smiley, Friend of The Soul Food Museum, being honored by Chef Willhoite

Friend of Soul Food Museum – Bern Nadette Stanis (better known as Thelma Evans on popular TV show "Good Times") with Chef Willhoite

Singer/Songwriter/Chef Isaac Hayes

New Orleans Chef Paul Prudhomme

Dorothy Height – Civil Rights & Social
Services Advocate Civil Rights
Served six decades with The National
Council of Negro Women;
Developed the Black Family Reunion
Celebration in Washington, D.C.

Martin Luther King, III, son of
Leader Martin Luther King, Jr.
Continues the legacy of Civil
Rights Activism worldwide

Chef Willhoite and his mother whom he honors
for her support, inspiration & encouragement.

AFTER THOUGHTS...

KEEPING SOUL FOOD ALIVE – BACK TO THE GARDEN & UNITY IN THE BLACK FAMILY

We must get back to the basics – to honoring that which God gave us in the beginning – an Eden, a place of perfect joy and bliss. From the cradle of civilization, Africa, came so much of how our lives have evolved – agriculturally, economically, spiritually, and finally how our food ways have transformed into what we have come to know as African American Soul Food.

Freed slaves accumulated roughly 15 million acres of land across the United States, most of it in the south. Generally, it was used for farming. By 1920 there were 925,000 black owned farms, representing approximately 14% of all farms in the U.S.

Our enslaved ancestors nurtured and worked the land, the soil -- to create foods that kept our people healthy and strong. This strength helped four generations of people to survive torture, separation from family, malnourishment, and a tearing away of the spirit that would have eliminated most people. It still pains me deeply when I envision my great great grandparents being dragged through dirt and brush, not knowing what was happening to them. They were chained like animals and dragged to a point of no return. For unending weeks, they were bound together in the bottom of filthy ships, wallowing in their own body fluids and almost starving to death. And that was only the beginning. For two hundred more years, those who survived birthed children who had no memory of their true homeland, the land of their ancestors – Africa. But what they did have inside of them was spirit memory, like muscle memory – a memory that kept the knowledge, skills and ways of their people. As I grew up, I saw that spirit in my mother and grandmother. My mother taught me everything that has kept me strong, determined and unstoppable in reaching my dreams. My grandmother taught me to love the land from which we became healthy and happy. From the land, we can grow good food – food for the soul. We then have an obligation to teach those who come behind us to do the same thing. Then, if we are blessed enough for this to continue, our families for generations to come will love the food from the land as we do and will come together in union to celebrate the land, the family, the love.

There is an African Proverb, which says, ***"If you want to go quickly, you go alone. If you want to go far, go together.*** From this juncture in our African American journey, we still have so far to go. But often out of adversity grows opportunity...

85

IMPORTANCE OF COOPERATIVES IN OUR COMMUNITIES

Over time following the emancipation of slaves in 1865, the 600,000 Black farmers diminished to less than 50,000 (1975). To help save the land some farmers formed cooperatives. As African American moved to northern cities during the Great Migration, cooperatives formed to aid workers in other various trades.

From 1880 – 1920 there were only a handful of Black Cooperatives in the U.S. Many groups that wanted to work together to become self-sufficient did so at the risk of being harassed, threatened or even killed because their unity was a threat to the white mainstream. It was not unusual for white vigilantes to burn down Black cooperative businesses, and entire towns. Some, however, managed to survive and even thrive:

- 1865-1883 - CHESAPEAKE MARINE RAILWAY and DRY DOCK COMPANY SHIPYARD - Baltimore, Maryland
- 1880's - BLACK COOPERATIVE VILLAGES near Birmingham, Alabama
- 1880's - BLACK COOPERATIVE COTTON GIN - Stewart's Station, Alabama
- 1897 - COLEMAN MANUFACTURING COMPANY - Concord, North Carolina
- 1901 – MERCANTILE COOPERATIVE COMPANY
- 1918 – NEGRO COOPERATIVE GUILD
- 1919 – CITIZENS CO-OPERATIVE STORES
- 1920 - UNITED NEGRO IMPROVEMENT ASSOCIATION'S "BLACK STAR LINE" and "NEGRO FACTORIES"
- 1927 – COLORED MERCHANTS SOCIETY
- 1930 – CONSUMER COOPERATIVE
- 1930 – AGRICULTURAL COOPERATIVE
- 1930 – YOUNG NEGROES' COOPERATIVE LEAGUE
- 1930-1940 – EASTERN CAROLINA COUNCIL FEDERATION

From the 1920s to 1960 Blacks progressed very slowly in building successful Black Cooperatives. However, in the 1960's a seed was regerminated to encourage the development of Black Cooperatives. It was one of the core components of the Civil Rights movement. Cooperatives have offered African Americans the opportunity to expand their production, to diversity their crops, and better market their produce in agriculture.[31] The primary goal of cooperatives is to show self-sufficiency. All members of cooperatives have equal interest and the goal is not to get rich but to meet basic human needs by contributing equally to a pre-determined goal. Those who felt that this concept was a very practical choice for making their enterprises work, came together with those of similar interests to grow food, to provide community services, to save money, to build cooperative farmland, and more.

- 1966 – FREEDOM QUILTING BEE (HANDCRAFT COOPERATION)
- 1967 – FEDERATION OF SOUTHERN COOPERATIVES
- 1997 – DAWSON COOPERATIVE DAWSON, GA
- WORKERS OWNED COOPERATIVE
- 2009 – MANDELA FOODS COOPERATIVE WEST OAKLAND, CA

That which we control, we truly own. Collective ownership will help many African Americans to reach a level of success in business working in unity. There are still challenges to getting there and we must continue to educate each other on how to reach this goal.

And you may be asking yourself, *"What in the world does any of this have to do with soul food"*. Well, I hoped to drive home the point that soul food has never been just about food. It is about all that we have moved through on our four-hundred-year journey, all that we strive to achieve, and all that we wish to leave for generations to follow us – just as our ancestors left their lessons for us. Just like the recipes that our ancestors left us – they didn't write them down, they didn't spell out every measurement, but they delivered the message loud and clear. We must feed our souls with all that makes us who we truly are as we continue to nourish our bodies with food that is healthy, but that also continues to bring us joy and unity.

My hope is that I have shared valuable information via this virtual tour of the history of the African American soul food story, and that you have learned more about our many contributions in the food and hospitality industry. Knowledge is power, and that power must be a shared power like the combined energy from an electrical power plant.

My journey will continue even after I have penned the last word in this book because our struggle continues, and I will never stop working to make a significant contribution in any way that I possibly can. Stay tuned for volumes to come with more history, more stories, and incredible knowledge that will be food for the soul.

---

[31] American Greetings, "Our Voices", Cleveland, Ohio.

*I believe in the aromas and flavors that simmer deep in
the kitchens of our memories.*

*I believe in soul food; I believe in the power to feed the body
and nourish the spirit.*

*I love how it sounds, rolling off my tongue –
Ham hocks, black-eyed peas, grits, cornbread, and collard greens*

American Greeting Card Quote.

ACKNOWLEDGMENTS

This is for you!

For over 40 years, I have been on a mission to tell the story of our people's 400-year journey. I could not have done this alone. I would like to thank all those whom God and the spirit of our ancestors have put in my path as I have traveled throughout the United States. I have been searching for the untold stories about soul food, and have met those who have contributed to the advancement of culinary arts, hospitality, and agriculture in America and throughout the world. There are far too many to name one by one, but there are a few people who have stood by me, encouraged me and guided me. There are over 8 billion people on the planet earth, but God and the spirit of our ancestors chose *you* to be in my life – to give your love and support, and for that reason I am blessed. I will be forever grateful to those who have inspired me, motivated me and educated me to be the best man I could be (*I am that I am*). My mother and grandmother did so much of that for me.

As an African American Chef, Historian and Soul Food Guru, I stand on the shoulders of those in our industry that came before me; that took courage and tenacity. Many young people have reached out to me to be their mentor; every successful entrepreneur needs one. Thank you very much, George Andrews for continuing to guide me as I continue my journey. You have been an extraordinary mentor for me. We all have a story, a voice to be heard. The world needs to hear your stories and know your name. As long as a living person calls out your name, you shall never die. You will live on through the contributions that you give to the world.

There was a book that I really needed to read. It had not yet been written, so I wrote it. I thank and respect those who have hailed me as one of the leading food, hospitality and agriculture researchers, but I simply remain your humble servant.

The Soul Food Museum is truly a ***Rite of Passage***; it illuminates the spirit and imagination for all of us who partake. We must all find new ways to teach, to learn, to uplift, and to pass knowledge on to those who will come behind us.

CHEF KENNETH WILLHOITE

CONTACT INFORMATION

Chef Willhoite is available for book signings, public speaking engagements, and conferences to share his expertise in African American culinary history, healthy eating initiatives (related to diabetes, cancer, strokes, heart disease, and HIV/AIDS).

The Soul Food Museum continues to accept historical African American soul food artifacts to add to this on-going collection. Feel free to contact Chef Willhoite:

Website: www.soulfoodmuseum.org
E-Mail Address: drwillhoite@yahoo.com

Phone: 678-508-9478

BIBLIOGRAPHY

African American Food Service: <u>BLACK VOICES.</u> "10 Black Chefs That Are Changing the Food World as We Know It". Mar 28, 2014

Baltimore City Public Schools: Social Studies Lesson 34. "African Americans and the Seafood Industry of the Chesapeake Bay" MUSEUM CONNECTION: LABOR and THE BLACK EXPERIENCE, <u>https://www.bcpss.org/bbcswebdav/institution/ Resources/An%20African%20American%20Journey/Lesson_34.pdf</u>

Boyd, Kristin "Blacks Carry on the Soul Food Tradition. February 6, 2011. The Reading Eagle Magazine

Brown, Stacia "The Untold History of African American Cookbooks". October 27, 2015. The New Republic Magazine

Carmichael, Rodney "Soul-Saving Mission", Creative Loafing Magazine. May 5, 2016

Carver, Helen Bush and Williams, Mary T. COUNTRIES AND THEIR CULTURES – CREOLES. World Culture Encyclopedia Dennis,

ChickenBoneBeach.org http://www.chickenbonebeach.org;#sthash.jAMj7XpJ.dpuf

Dennis, Chef B. J. "OLDWAYS – Inspiring Good Health Through Cultural Food Traditions". September 2016 Gullah Geechee Blog <u>https://oldwayspt.org/blog/ want-learn-about-gullah-geechee-cuisine-look-no-further-chef-bj-dennis</u>

Dewan, Shaila "Celebrity and Showmanship on a Soul Food Menu", New York Times News, FEB. 14, 2008

Dickerson, Jessica HISTORICAL DOCUMENTARIES: *"Booker's Place", 1966* – Chronicles the indignities suffered by waiter Booker Wright.

Hurt, Byron "Soul Food Junkies", Independent Lens Video 2012

International Slavery Museum Magazine "Slavery Diet and Food Production". http://www.liverpoolmuseums.org.uk/ism/slavery/archaeology/caribbean/caribbean2.

Libguides.sunysccc.edu, "Origins of Soul Food"

McClurg, Heather "6 African American Scientist and Their Contributions to Agriculture and Food", Monsanto Corporate Engagement

McKibben, Beth "The Real Roots of Southern Cuisine.". Deep Roots Magazine. December 3, 2012

Miller, Adrian SOUL FOOD - The Surprising Story of an American Cuisine – One Plate at a Time. North Carolina: University of North Carolina, 2013

Museum of African American History "BLACK ENTREPRENEURS OF EIGHTEENTH & NINETEENTH CENTURIES" - A partnership with the Federal Reserve Bank of Boston, Boston and Nantucket

Nembhard, Jessica Gordon Collective Courage – History of African American Cooperative Economic Thought and Practice. Pennsylvania State University Press 2014

Nodjimbadem, Katie "What 200 Years of African-American Cookbooks Reveal About How We Stereotype Food". Smithsonian.com

Pinchin, Karen "How Slaves Shaped American Cooking", National Geographic Magazine. March 1, 2014

Pittsburg Post "Grandma Explains It All – Why Do We Eat Black-Eyed Peas for New Year's". Gazettehttp://wgno.com/2015/12/29/grandma-explains-it-all-why-do-we-eat-black-eyed-peas-for-new-years/ February 23, 2006

Ruane, Laura "Black Owned Restaurants Nourished the Activist Soul", USA TODAY, Feb. 18, 2014

Sambira, Jocelyne "Slave trade: How African foods influenced modern American cuisine". AfricaRenewal Online

Sanna, Ellyn "American Cooking Library – Culture, Tradition, and History: African American". Consultant: The Culinary Institute of America, Mason Crest Publishers, 2005

Smith, Andrew "U S SLAVE - The Confederacy's Salt Famine". WordPress Blog, April 15, 2013

Stanford University School of Medicine "Ethnogeniology". https://geriatrics.stanford.edu/ethnomed/african_american/fund/health_history/longevity.html

Today.com "Blacks Carry on Soul Food Tradition". February 6, 2011http://www.today.com/food/why-these-5-foods-are-eaten-good-luck-new-year-t61496

Woods, Chef Marvin "Coastal Cuisine: African Diaspora Meets the South". Jet Magazine, Feb. 20, 2015

Yetman, Norman R. – Editor "When I was a Slave – Memoirs from the Slave Narrative Collection". Dover Thrift Publications. 2002

Zuckerman, Catherine National Geographic Magazine. 5 African Foods You Thought Were American. September 21, 2016

Index

Printed in the United States
By Bookmasters